THE NEW

LIMITED PARTNERSHIP INVESTMENT ADVISOR A GUIDE TO SUPERIOR RETURNS THROUGH TODAY'S LIMITED PARTNERSHIPS

G. TIMOTHY HAIGHT

PROBUS PUBLISHING COMPANY
Chicago, Illinois

Haight, G. Timothy.
   The new limited partnership investment advisor.

   Includes index.
   1. Limited partnership—United States.
   2. Investments—Law and legislation—United States.
   3. Limited partnership—Taxation—United States.
   4. Investments—Taxation—Law and legislation—
United States. I. Title.
KF1380.H35   1987   346.73'0682   87-2491
                         347.306682

ISBN 0-917253-71-X

Library of Congress Catalog Card No. 87–2491

Printed in the United States of America

1 2 3 4 5 6 7 8 9 0

DEDICATION

This book is dedicated to my wife
  Ann

Preface

If you have recently read an offering memorandum for a limited partnership, you may have been left with the impression that these documents are intended to be confusing. Although syndicators do not deliberately attempt to confuse potential investors, that is frequently what they achieve. Understanding limited partnerships can often be a difficult task, even for the most seasoned investment advisor. The complexities of today's investment vehicles coupled with those of today's ever-changing tax laws require investors to keep their knowledge of investing up to the minute. What is needed is a systematic approach to the evaluation of investment alternatives using the techniques of modern financial analysis.

The purpose of *The New Limited Partnership Investment Advisor: A Guide to Superior Returns through Today's Limited Partnerships* is to provide readers with the background necessary to properly evaluate limited partnership investment opportunities using the techniques of modern financial analysis. It will enable investors to better assess the economic merits of an offering in order to arrive at a correct decision regarding its purchase.

This book is divided into two sections. The first section deals primarily with the nature of limited partnership investments, their place in the investor's portfolio, and the financial concepts underlying the investment. This section also examines how to screen these investments by reading prospectuses.

The second section focuses on the particular types of limited partnerships available today. These include real estate, equipment leasing, oil and gas, research and development, mortgage, and the more exotic types of limited partnerships, such as horse syndication, motion pictures, orange groves, and cattle breeding. Each of these investments is examined in depth.

G. Timothy Haight

ACKNOWLEDGMENTS

The writing of this book was accomplished with the help of many who have given invaluable assistance. First, I thank my wife Ann, who has tirelessly labored over countless rewrites as my editor.

I express my gratitute to Probus Publishing Company, a constant source of encouragement througout this project.

I also thank three collegues who have been a source of encouragement througout the past decade and a half: Professor Frederick Amling, Professor of Finance at George Washington University, John J. Hampton, Dean of Seton Hall University, and Professor Art Holt, of Towson State University.

A note of special thanks goes to several of my friends in the Baltimore business community who have aided me in my research effort. In particular, I thank Jay Atkinson (Baker Watts), Robert F. Boyd (Mercantile Safe Deposit and Trust Company), Gregg Bryant (Coldwell Banker), Burland East (Alex Brown & Sons), Rick Faint, Jr. (Persona Care), Charles Famula (Coyne & Mc Clean), Matt Glenn (Legg Mason), Skip Johnson (Provident Bank of Maryland), John Kelly (Merrill Lynch), Joseph M. Knott (Joseph M. Knott, Inc.), Andrew Long (Thomson-CGR Medical Corporation), L. Gary Owens (Mercantile-Safe Deposit and Trust Company), James Plitt (Clifton Trust Bank), Georges F. Rocourt (Mercantile-Safe Deposit and Trust Company), Glenn Ross (Mercantile-Safe Deposit and Trust Company), and Alvin Schugam for their assistance.

I also thank my colleagues at the University of Baltimore, for providing an atmosphere conducive to research. In particular, I thank President Mebane Turner, Dean Sydney Stern, and Professors Deborah Ford, John Silberman and Kenneth Smith for their encouragement. Thanks also goes to my research assistant, Douglas R. McMenamin for his assistance.

CONTENTS

Contents

Contents

Contents

Chapter 1

An Introduction To Limited Partnerships

It is easy to understand why limited partnerships have become so popular in recent years. These partnerships can offer investors returns superior to those achieved by stocks and bonds. They can offer tax-free cash distributions during the life of the limited partnership, as well as the opportunity to share in significant cash distributions when the partnership is terminated.

The attractiveness of limited partnerships as an investment has been further enhanced as a result of the 1986 Tax Reform Act. This chapter presents the many benefits derived from the passage of the Tax Reform Act. First, however, we will examine the functions and some of the general requirements of income-oriented limited partnerships.

AN OVERVIEW OF LIMITED PARTNERSHIPS

Limited partnerships are created to acquire assets for investment purposes. These partnerships are actually comprised of two types of partners: general and limited. The *general partners* are responsible for carrying out the day-to-day responsibilities of the business and have unlimited liability. In return for a fee, the general partners provide professional expertise in actively managing the partnership's assets and make all of the business decisions. In addition, the general partners assume unlimited liability on behalf of the partnership.

The *limited partners* provide most of the capital required to fund the operations of the partnership. They are not permitted to engage in the business activities of the partnership, and their liability is usually limited to the amount that they contribute and/or pledge.

The partnership itself is not a taxable entity; it serves as a conduit in which profits and losses flow through to the individual level. These profits and losses can be allocated to each partner differently, as long as there is a sound business purpose for doing so. In return for the limited partners' equity contribution, the partnership allocates most of the profits and cash distributions to them, based upon a predetermined sharing arrangement stipulated in the partnership agreement.

REQUIREMENTS FOR CLASSIFICATION AS A LIMITED PARTNERSHIP

The IRS has recently directed its efforts in challenging the business form of many limited partnership investments. It has been argued that these businesses are partnerships in name only and that they should really be taxed as corporations.

IRS regulations state that an organization will be taxed as a partnership unless it possesses more corporate than noncorporate characteristics (see table 1.1). Two of these, "organization consists of Associates" and "having as an objective the intent to conduct business and divide the profits therefrom," are shared by both partnerships and corporations; therefore, these characteristics are not considered. If an organization fails to qualify as a limited partnership by meeting the requirements, then the entity will be classified as an association and treated as a corporation for tax purposes.

Table 1.1
Screening Characteristics
Used by IRS to Determine
Tax Treatment of Limited Partnerships
(Corporation Versus Partnership)

1. Formed for the purpose of carrying out a business to earn a profit
2. Organization consists of associates
3. Continuity of life
4. Centralized management
5. Limited liability
6. Free transferability of interests

The Internal Revenue Service has put forth guidelines that enable partnerships to be treated as such for tax purposes. If followed, these guidelines ensure that these entities are treated as partnerships by the Internal Revenue Service.

Treatment as a partnership for tax purposes is even more important under the Tax Reform Act of 1986. For the first time in decades the top individual tax rate (28 percent) will be lower than the top corporate rate (34 percent). Thus the loss of this favorable tax status would undoubtedly result in a lower after tax return.

INCREASED LIQUIDITY OF LIMITED PARTNERSHIPS

The emergence of a secondary market for limited partnership units has provided liquidity for individual investors who wish to trade their interests. Before the development of this market, limited partners were locked into their investment until such time as the general partners wished to dissolve the partnership. The traditional limited partnership's lack of liquidity prompted various firms to enter the after market.

Limited partnership units are now being actively marketed by specialized brokerage firms. However, the sellers of partnership units may experience significant losses. Table 1.2 lists various market makers in limited partnership interests.

**Table 1.2
Limited Partnership
Market Makers**

Equity Resources Corporation (Massachusetts)

Liquidity Fund (California)

Oppenheimer & Bigelow (New York)

MacKenzie Securities and Repurchase (California)

Partnership Securities Exchange (California)

Raymond James & Associates (Florida)

Realty Repurchase (California)

Source: *Forbes*, November 3, 1986. pp. 258-260.

One of the first responses to the limited partnership units' lack of liquidity was the reaction of the master limited partnership (MLP). These MLP units provide the investor with liquidity since they are actively traded on the New York and American Exchanges, as well as in the over-the-counter market.

There are three types of Master Limited Partnerships: roll-up, roll-in, and roll-out. A roll-up MLP raises capital through the issuance of securities (master limited partnership units) and uses these funds to acquire the interests of several smaller limited partnerships.

This type of MLP was used extensively in the oil and gas industry during the early 1970s and is used in the real estate industry today. Many smaller illiquid limited partnerships were combined or "rolled up" into master limited partnerships. In some instances the sponsors packaged marginal oil and gas limited partnerships into these MLPs.

Roll-in MLP uses proceeds from primary offerings to purchase new or additional investment assets themselves rather than limited partnership interests. These MLPs use the market as a funding source for its growth objectives. The investor in roll-in MLPs should carefully scrutinize its acquisition and management fees to ensure that they are not excessive.

Roll-out MLP is similar to a corporate divestiture. Here, a corporation will create a master limited partnership and sell it its assets. Typically the sponsor corporation will also be the managing corporation. The roll-out MLP is the ideal for those corporations whose underlying asset value exceeded their stocks' market value. Furthermore, for the first time in recent memory individual tax rates are lower than corporate tax rates. Thus, corporations can increase their after-tax return by spinning off MLPs.

These new innovations will provide the limited partnership investors with markets for their individual units as well as providing them with the most current information relating to the market value of their units. The ability of these partnerships to be actively traded will be one of the larger contributing factors for the continued success of these investments.

We will now examine the extent to which these partnerships have gained popularity in recent years.

Chapter 1

GROWTH OF LIMITED PARTNERSHIPS

Investors are increasingly turning their attention to limited partnerships due to the success of such partnerships as investments. As shown in table 1.3, over $18 billion worth of limited partnership interests were sold in both 1984 and 1985. Partnership sales are expected to exceed the $18 billion level again in 1986.[1]

These limited partnership units can be sold to investors through either private or public offerings. Private offerings involve the sale of units on a limited or restricted basis. Usually, these sales will be to "sophisticated" investors through the use of a private placement memorandum. Each investor may be required to invest several thousands of dollars over a period of several years.

A public offering of a limited partnership requires that investors receive a prospectus at the start of the selling effort. Unlike private offerings, public limited partnerships may require a single payment of as little as $1,000. Public limited partnerships allow small investors to pool their funds and invest in assets often beyond their individual financial reach. A close inspection of table 1.3 reveals that in 1985 almost 61 percent of total limited partnership sales were public offerings, compared to 1984 where only 44 percent of the total represented public offerings.

This increase in public limited partnerships is not surprising. In contrast to private offerings which are often shelter-oriented, public limited partnerships are typically income-oriented. The most popular public limited partnerships investments were in real estate, where total public sales increased from $5,686,000,000 in 1984 to $8,062,000,000 in 1985. In fact, public real estate limited partnerships accounted for almost 70 percent of the total public partnership sales in

[1] "Limited Partnership Sales Summary 1985," *The Stanger Review*, Robert A. Stanger & Company, p. 6.

Table 1.3
Total Partnership Market
($ in millions)

	1984 (1)	1985 (2)	Percent change 1984-1985
Real Estate			
Public	$ 5,686	$ 8,062	41.8%
Private	5,308	4,600	-13.3%
Total	$ 10,944	$ 12,662	15.2%
Oil & Gas			
Public	$ 1,694	$ 1,856	9.6%
Private	1,674	430	-74.3%
Total	$ 3,368	$ 2,286	-32.1%
Equipment Leasing			
Public	$ 478	$ 557	16.4%
Private	158	200	26.3%
Total	$ 636	$ 757	18.9%
R&D/Venture Capital			
Public	$ 99	$ 159	60.8%
Private	615	850	38.3%
Total	$ 714	$ 1,009	41.4%
Miscellaneous			
Public	$ 444	$ 915	106.0%
Private	2,742	1,330	-51.5%
Total	$ 3,186	$ 2,245	-29.5%

Table 1.3 (Continued)
Total Partnership Market
($ in millions)

	1984 (1)	*1985 (2)*	*Percent change 1984-1985*
Total Public	$ 8,401	$ 11,549	37.5%
Total Private	10,497	7,410	-29.4%
Total Market	$ 18,898	$ 18,959	0.3%

[1] 1984 private closings annualized based on Form D filings between April 1, 1984 and December 31, 1984.

[2] Actual private closings from January 1 through October 31, 1985 plus estimated private closings for November and December 1985.

Source: *The Stanger Review*, "Limited Partnership Sales Summary 1985," p. 1.

1985. Oil and gas limited partnerships were the second most popular public programs, followed by equipment leasing.

Table 1.4 presents the volume of sales of real estate, oil and gas, and equipment leasing public (income-oriented) limited partnerships during 1984 and 1985. As shown in the table, these limited partnerships are becoming increasingly popular. Total income-oriented investments increased by over 56 percent form 1984 to 1985. Public real estate limited partnerships enjoyed widespread popularity from income-oriented investors, increasing by almost 74 percent from 1984 to 1985. Investment in income-oriented equipment leasing limited partnerships also grew at a rate of over 34 percent during this period. However, income-oriented oil and gas programs grew at a more modest rate of 16.2 percent from 1984 to 1985.

Table 1.4
Public Partnership in
Income-Oriented Investments
($ in millions)

	1984	1985	Percent change 1984-1985	1985 Market share
Real Estate				
Unleveraged	$ 1,953.3	$ 2,890.1	48.0%	25.0%
Mortgage Loans	938.7	1,901.6	102.6%	16.5
FREIT's [1]	413.0	948.3	129.6%	8.2
Total	$ 3,305.0	$ 4,740.0	73.7%	49.7%
Oil & Gas				
Income	$ 985.5	$ 253.7	-74.3%	2.2%
Combination	19.0	0.0	-110.0%	0.0
MLPs [2]	211.5	1,159.4	448.2%	10.1
Total	$ 1,216.0	$ 1,413.1	16.2%	12.3%
Equipment Leasing				
Income-Oriented	$ 346.1	$ 466.4	34.8%	4.0%
Total	$ 4,867.1	$ 7,619.5	56.5%	66.0%

[1] Finite-life Real Estate Investment Trusts
[2] Master Limited Partnerships

Source: *The Stanger Review*, "Limited Partnership Sales Summary 1985," p.3.

Chapter 1

Table 1.5 presents the volume of sales of real estate, oil and gas, equipment leasing, and miscellaneous shelter-oriented limited partnerships during 1984 and 1985. As shown in table 1.5 shelter-oriented public limited partnerships experienced sluggish growth between 1984 and 1985 due mainly to the uncertainties surrounding tax reform.

Table 1.5
Public Partnership in
Shelter-Oriented Investments
($ in millions)

	1984	1985	Percent change 1984-1985	1985 Market share
Real Estate				
Leveraged	$ 2,380.9	$ 2,321.7	- 2.4%	20.1%
Oil & Gas				
Drilling	$ 414.3	$ 370.7	-10.5%	3.2%
Royalty/ Completion	63.8	72.7	14.0%	0.6%
Total	$ 478.1	$ 443.4	- 7.4%	3.8%
Equipment Leasing				
Shelter-oriented	$ 132.1	$ 90.3	-31.6%	0.8%
Miscellaneous	$ 543.1	$ 1,074.3	97.8%	9.3%
Total	$ 3,534.2	$ 3,929.7	11.2%	34.0%

Source: *The Stanger Review*, "Limited Partnership Sales Summary 1985," p. 3.

TAX REFORM ACT OF 1986

The Tax Reform Act of 1986 further enhances the desirability of limited partnerships, by ensuring that newly-created partnerships will be based on the underlying economic value of their assets. We will address some of the more important benefits of investing in income-oriented limited partnerships as a result of the act in the following paragraphs.

Lower Marginal Rates

First, the lowering of marginal tax rates will increase the after-tax return of these investment vehicles. The Tax Reform Act of 1986 reduces the top individual rate from 50 percent to 28 percent beginning in 1988. Furthermore, the 15 tax brackets were replaced by 2 brackets. Table 1.6 presents the 1988 tax rate schedule for single taxpayers and married couples filing joint returns.

Table 1.6
Taxable Income
1988 Tax Brackets

Single filer	Married couples filing jointly	Tax rate
up to $17,850	up to $29,750	15%
over $17,850	over $29,750	28%

Note: For single taxpayers who have taxable income which exceeds$43,150 ($71,900 for couples filing joint returns) a surtax is imposed to phase out the benefits of the 15 percent tax rate and personal exemption.

Chapter 1

To understand the importance of a taxpayer's marginal tax rate on an investment decision, consider the following example. An investor is contemplating the purchase of either a corporate bond yielding eight percent or a municipal bond yielding six percent. Assume that both of these bonds are of the highest quality rated AAA and will mature at the same time.

The investor's decision is not unlike those many investors face daily. The choice is between a fully taxable corporate bond yielding eight percent and a tax-exempt bond yielding six percent. In this instance, the decision should be based on the investor's after-tax return. In the case of the municipal bond, the after-tax return is six percent, since a municipal bond's interest income is tax exempt.

To determine the after-tax return on the corporate bond, it is first necessary to determine the investor's marginal tax rate. If we assume that the marginal tax rate is 28 percent, then the investor's after-tax return on the corporate bond is only 5.76 percent (8% X (1 - 0.28)).

Based on the above analysis, the investor's correct decision would be to select the municipal bond, despite the corporate bond's higher before-tax yield of eight percent versus six percent. This is because the after-tax return favors the municipal bond due to the investor's high marginal tax rate.

If the investor's marginal tax rate were under 15 percent, the corporate bond would produce an after-tax yield of 6.8 percent (8% X (1 - 0.15)). In that instance, the investor would purchase the corporate bond, since its after-tax return (6.8%) is greater than that of the tax-exempt bond (6%).

Thus, it is very important to consider the after-tax rate of return on an investment in order to determine its full impact. Since investors' marginal tax rates affect their after-tax return on an investment, they must incorporate it into their decision-making processes. In fact, individuals' exposure to taxes must be considered in all investment decisions.

Limited Partnership Treatment of Cash Distributions

Second, the Tax Reform Act of 1986 continues to treat limited partners' cash distributions favorably. To the extent that these distributions are viewed as a return of invested capital, they are taxed. However, this will reduce the investors' tax basis. This topic will be addressed in chapters 8 and 10.

A corporation must pay taxes when it earns a profit. If it then wishes to distribute some of the profits to its shareholders, it will usually pay a dividend. These dividends are then taxed again when the individuals receive them. The Tax Reform Act repeals the $200 dividend exclusion ($100 for single tax payers) and thus subjects all corporate dividends to taxation. Thus, one of the chief disadvantages of the corporate form is the exposure to double taxation.

On the other hand, in a limited partnership cash may be distributed to investors without exposing the them to taxes on the entire amount. This will occur if the partnership fails to show "book profits" (we will explain this concept further in chapter 3). The result is that investors will often receive funds without incurring any immediate tax liability.

Renewed Emphasis on Income-oriented Limited Partnerships

Third, the passage of the Tax Reform Act refocuses our attention on the economic value of an investment rather than its tax sheltering characteristics. Prior to the passage of the 1986 Tax Reform Act, investors often entered into shelter-oriented limited partnerships with the primary purpose of generating losses to offset otherwise taxable income. These interests could generate losses to offset an individual's other taxable income. It was the limited partnership's conduit feature that allowed individuals to either postpone, reduce, or escape taxation by acquiring limited partnership interests. Consequently, shelter promoters pumped up front-end fees, increasing losses which were then written off against investor's earned income. Since the government was picking up as much as half the tab, many investors seemed unconcerned.

The loss motive behind many shelter-oriented limited partnerships was dealt a serious blow with the passage of the "passive loss" provisions of the Tax Reform Act of 1986, in which Congress sought to restrict the use of passive losses as a tax avoidance technique. The Tax Reform Act defines passive losses as losses incurred in activities in which the individual investor does not materially participate. This requires the investors to be involved in the daily operations of the business on a continuous basis. By definition, holders of limited partnership interests are not materially participating in the partnership. Therefore, losses generated from investing in a limited partnership (with the exception of oil and gas working interests) would be categorized as passive losses, and thus could not be used to offset wages or portfolio income.

Investors who purchase limited partnerships interests after the Bill's enactment will only be able to apply their share of these partnership losses against other passive income. Thus, they will not be allowed to apply these losses against earned or portfolio income.

This provision of the Tax Reform Act of 1986 will increase the desirability of owning income-oriented limited partnerships, since passive losses can be used to offset income from these investments. Thus, those who previously entered into shelter-oriented limited partnerships can enhance the after-tax return on these income-oriented limited partnerships.

The Tax Reform Act of 1986 provides transition rules for those who purchased shelter-oriented limited partnerships prior to its enactment. For these investors, the passive loss rules will be phased in over a period of four years. When this provision takes full affect (1991), losses generated from investing in pre-1987 limited partnership will only be allowed to offset other passive income (see table 1.7 for the yearly phase-in schedule).

Table 1.7
Passive Loss
Phase-In Schedule

Taxable year	Percentage allowed
1986	100%
1987	65%
1988	40%
1989	20%
1990	10%
1991 and thereafter	0%

Note: The phase-in provision affects only those individuals who entered into shelter-oriented activities prior to 1987.

To illustrate the impact of the passive loss rules, suppose an investor in 1986 purchased a shelter-oriented limited partnership in which he expected to incur losses of $10,000 for each of the next six years (including 1986). The amount of losses that he could write off against earned income (and dividend and interest income) would be determined as shown in table 1.8.

Table 1.8
Illustration of Passive Loss Phase-In
Assuming $10,000 for 6 Years

Taxable year	Year's loss	Percentage allowed	Allowable losses
1986	$10,000	100%	$10,000
1987	10,000	65%	6,500
1988	10,000	40%	4,000
1989	10,000	20%	2,000
1990	10,000	10%	1,000
1991	10,000	0%	0

Note: Under the passive loss provisions, disallowed passive losses can be carried forward to offset other passive income or to applied to gains realized upon the disposition of property.

Chapter 1

ROLE OF ALTERNATIVE MINIMUM TAX

First introduced by Congress as part of the Tax Reform Act of 1968, the alternative minimum tax was designed specifically for those individuals whose tax liabilities had been significantly reduced by use of so-called tax preference items. The Tax Reform Act of 1986 further tightens the provisions of the 1968 Act by increasing the number of tax preference items.

Thus, tax preference items include certain tax-exempt interest from post-August 7, 1986-issued securities, as well as other items previously excluded. The alternative minimum tax has additional implications for those investors who continue to show passive losses from shelter-oriented programs, regardless of when the investment was entered into. Under the Tax Reform Act of 1986 passive losses are an item of tax preference. Hence, investors who were counting on continued deductions due to the phase-in of the passive loss provisions must treat all of the losses as items of tax preference when calculating the alternative minimum tax.

Under this method, the taxpayer is required compute what is called the alternative minimum taxable income (AMTI). This is accomplished by adding the dollar amount of tax preferences to the taxpayer's adjusted gross income and then reducing that total by the amount of alternative tax itemized deductions.

Once we obtain the alternative minimum taxable income, we then reduce that figure by the exemption amount to arrive at the excess alternative minimum taxable income. The exemption amount is $40,000 for couples filing jointly, $20,000 for couples filing separately, and $30,000 for people filing as single. The exemption would be reduced by 25 percent of the amount that AMTI exceeds $150,000 ($112,500 for couples filing separately and $75,000 for single filers) for joint returns. Thus, the excess alternative minimum taxable income would then be taxed at a rate of 21 percent.

In essence, many of the tax advantages created by Congress not only stimulate investments but also allow many wealthy individuals to escape taxation partially or completely. This politically unacceptable consequence was the main focus of the alternative minimum tax. Taxpayers who would otherwise greatly reduce their tax liability through the use of certain tax deductions (tax preferences) are required to recalculate their tax liability using the alternative minimum tax method.

SUMMARY

Limited partnerships have enjoyed widespread acceptance as a business form. They consist of both general and limited partners. The general partners are responsible for managing the partnership's assets and assume unlimited liability, while the limited partners provide most of the capital and have limited liability. In order for a business entity to qualify as a limited partnership for tax purposes, the IRS requires that limited partnerships possess certain noncorporate characteristics.

Secondary markets for limited partnership units are now being created to facilitate free exchange among investors. This will provide limited partners with a degree of liquidity unavailable in the past.

Limited partnerships have experienced rapid growth in the 1980s, with public programs providing small investors with opportunities to acquire assets by pooling their funds. The emphasis has shifted away from shelter-oriented programs to income-oriented limited partnerships.

Income-oriented limited partnerships are expected to be even more popular with the passage of the Tax Reform Act of 1986. The lowering of marginal rates, continued preferential treatment of cash distributions, and elimination of shelter-oriented limited partnerships through the adoption of the passive loss provisions will further enhance the attractiveness of income-oriented limited partnerships.

The alternative minimum tax was enacted by Congress as part of the Tax Reform Act of 1968. The Tax Reform Act of 1986 expands the list of tax preference items. The law requires individuals who would otherwise escape taxation through the use of certain tax deductions (tax preferences) to recompute their tax obligations using the alternative minimum tax method. The AMT method require taxpayers to compute their excess alternative minimum taxable income (EAMTI). Taxpayers are then required to pay a tax equal to 21 percent of the EAMTI less their regular tax liability.

Chapter 2

Revenue And Expense Characteristics Of Limited Partnerships

Understanding the origin and nature of revenue and expenses is the key to the proper selection of income-oriented limited partnership investments. This chapter presents the more important issues relating to the revenues as well as the types of expenses normally associated with these partnerships. First, we will focus on the revenue aspects of limited partnerships.

REVENUES

Income-oriented limited partnerships are often designed to provide high-yielding investments over an extended period of time. Since these partnerships are sometimes leveraged, the ability of a project to generate a sufficient cash flow to cover the debt service requirements and other operating expenses is essential to ensuring its success. Thus a proper determination of revenue sources and their current and future prospects will enable investors to more accurately assess the business risk of investments.

Since an investment's economic value will be based largely on the ability of the business in question to maintain and/or increase profit margins, the forces of supply and demand must be carefully assessed. Determining the underlying factors that affect the demand for a product or service may aid potential investors in judging its future prospects.

The revenue implications resulting from changes on the supply side must also be explored for each type of income-oriented investment under consideration. An investor must make an assessment of the likely competition, asking "Are there any barriers to prevent competitor's entries into this investment's market?" It is important to remember that supply often lags behind demand. For example, after the price of gasoline rose in the 1970s, the industry reacted by dramatically increasing the supply of petroleum. Marginal wells became profitable, due to the rise in the price of crude. Supply increased to meet the demand for oil. As a result, the rush to fulfill the demand glutted the market, and prices fell.

EXPENSES

Investors must determine whether the expected revenue from an income-oriented limited partnership is sufficient to cover its normal expenses and provide an attractive after-tax rate of return as well. Thus, in addition to the amount and stability of the partnership's revenue, investors must identify and forecast its expenses as well. These expenses include organizational, management and development, operating, and financial items.

Organizational and Syndication Expenses

Costs incurred in the organization of a partnership are not fully deductible in the year incurred. Section 709 of the Internal Revenue Code defines organizational expenses as "expenses which are incident to the creation of the partnership, chargeable to capital account, and of a character which, if expended incident to the creation of a partnership having an ascertainable life, would be amortizable over such life." Expenses fitting this definition can be amortized over a period of not less than 60 months. Ordinarily these expenses will include legal and accounting fees incident to the partnership organization and various filing fees.

Section 709 also requires the capitalization of certain syndication fees. Thus, while these expenses might necessitate immediate cash outlays, the requirement that they be capitalized delays their immediate deductibility. The code also prohibits the amortizing of certain other expenses. Included among these are costs incurred in issuing and marketing partnership units. Thus, while investors will not receive any immediate benefit in terms of deductions, they will be able to increase their basis in the limited partnership interest.

Management/Development Expenses

Fees paid to the general partners for their development and/or management of the business are referred to as management/development expenses. On occasion the IRS has taken the position that these are not expenses at all but merely cash distributions to the general partners. When that is the case, these fees represent cash outflows without the benefit of being a deductible item of the partnership.

Operating Expenses

Operating expenses are those expenses necessarily incurred in carrying on the activities of the partnership. Some examples of these expenses are materials, labor, maintenance, insurance, leasing fees, and property taxes. Each of these items should be carefully evaluated to determine whether they are likely to contribute to falling profit margins.

Depreciation Expenses

Purchases of fixed assets include buildings, machinery, and equipment. The costs of these fixed assets are often quite high, while their useful lives are sometimes short. The economic life of an asset is limited due to physical deterioration, technological obsolescence, or other causes. In recognition of this, taxpayers are permitted to write off, or *depreciate*, the costs of these assets over their useful lives.

Depreciation is a noncash periodic write-off against the cost of qualified property. The Economic Recovery Act of 1981 liberalized the depreciation laws by allowing assets to be written off over periods much shorter than their useful lives. The Tax Reform Act of 1986 revised the Accelerated Cost Recovery System (ACRS). The new ACRS, which categorizes depreciable property into eight asset classes, is presented in table 2.1. All assets placed in service after December 1986 must be depreciated using the new guidelines.

As shown in table 2.1, the Tax Reform Act of 1986 also extended the recovery period for depreciable real property (real estate) to 27.5 years for residential rental property, and 31.5 years for nonresidential real property and property with a depreciation range (ADR) midlife of 27.5 years or more.

The Tax Reform Act also requires investors to depreciate real estate using the straight-line depreciation method. This method produces equal yearly write-offs over the class life of the asset. Using the straight-line method, the yearly depreciation amount is found by dividing the cost of property acquired by its recovery period in years.

Table 2.1
Accelerated Cost Recovery System
Classes and Types of Property

Class	Property type
3-year 200% Class	This asset class includes personal property with a a depreciation range (ADR) midpoint of 4 years or less
5-year 200% Class	This asset class includes personal property with a depreciation range (ADR) midpoint of between 4.5 and 9.5 years. Included in this class are automobiles, light trucks, research and experimentation equipment, as well as other qualified technological equipment.
7-year 200% Class	This asset class includes certain real property with a depreciation range (ADR) midpoint of between 10 and 12.5 years, such as agricultural or horicultural structures, or property with no designated ADR midpoint.
10-year 200% Class	This asset class includes property with depreciation range (ADR) midpoint of between 16 and 19.5 years.
15-year 150% Class	This asset class includes property with depreciation range (ADR) midpoint of between 20 and 24.5 years.
20-year 150% Class	This asset class includes property with depreciation range (ADR) midpoint of 25 years or more, other than real property, with an depreciation range (ADR) midpoint equal to or greater than 27.5 years.
27.5-year Straight-Line Class	Residential real property.
31.5-year Straight-Line Class	Nonresidential real property.

FINANCING EXPENSES

Sometimes, in order to enhance the after-tax return on an investment, only part of the acquisition price will be financed with equity or capital contributed by the limited partners. The remainder of the required funds would be secured through debt. This use of debt is often referred to as *financial leverage*

The use of debt can be at either the partnership or the individual investor level. Regardless of which level leverage is employed, debt financing can enhance after-tax return of an investment. At the same time, however, it will also increase the investor's risk.

FINANCIAL LEVERAGE

The use of leverage can magnify the return that investors experience on their invested capital. If a particular investment possesses favorable financial leverage, the project's return on assets can be leveraged into an even higher return on the equity (the amount of capital contributed by the partners). Favorable financial leverage will usually exist when the return on an asset (income/investment) exceeds the cost of borrowed funds.

To understand the concept of favorable financial leverage, consider an investment that is expected to provide a yearly income of $10,000 before taxes. If acquisition costs were $100,000, then the return on assets would be 10 percent (income/assets) before taxes or 7.2 percent after taxes (10% X (1 - 28%) assuming that the investors are in the 28 percent tax bracket. If they put up all the money (no borrowed funds), their after-tax return on equity (invested cash) would also be 7.2 percent, since their equity would equal their total investment.

Suppose a bank is willing to lend investors $80,000 of the needed $100,000 at an interest rate of 8 percent per annum (interest only). They would therefore only have to put up $20,000 themselves. If they do this, what would their first year's after-tax return on equity be? Table 2.2 answers this question by illustrating the impact of leverage on their after-tax return on equity.

Since the investors' before-tax return on investment (10 percent) is greater than the cost of debt (8 percent), favorable financial leverage exists. Therefore their after-tax return on equity must increase from its unleveraged return of 7.2 percent. As Table 2.2 indicates, the investors' after-tax return on equity increases to 12.96 percent when they borrow 80 percent of the investment.

Table 2.2
Impact of Leverage on
Return on Equity
($20,000 Invested)

Total assets (investment)	$100,000
Debt (8% per annum interest rate)	80,000
Equity (Investor's contribution)	20,000
Return on investment (income/assets)	10%
Investor's marginal tax rate	28%
Total income (10% X total assets)	$ 10,000
Less: Cost of debt($80,000 X 8%)	6,400
Before-tax return on equity	3,600
Less: Taxes due	1,008
After-tax return on equity	2,592
Return on equity	$20,592 / $20,000 or 12.96%

What would happen if the investors increase the degree of financial leverage by borrowing 95 percent of the investment? Assuming that they could borrow the $95,000 at 8 percent, their after-tax return on equity would be calculated as in table 2.3.

Table 2.3 illustrates the impact of the additional leverage on the investors' after-tax return on equity. Their return on equity increases to 34.56 percent with borrowings of 95 percent of the investment value, versus 12.96 percent with debt equalling 80 percent of the investment.

Table 2.3
Impact of Leverage on
Return on Equity
($5,000 Invested)

Total assets (investment)	$100,000
Debt (per annum interest rate 8%)	95,000
Equity (investor's contribution)	5,000
Return on investment (income/assets)	10%
Investor's marginal tax rate	28%
Total income(10% X total assets)	$ 10,000
Less: Cost of debt ($95,000 X 8%)	7,600
Before-tax return on equity	2,400
Less: Taxes due	672
After-tax return on equity	$ 1,728
Return on equity	$1,728 / $5,000 or 34.56%

The use of additional debt can also be seen in figure 2.1. Here the investors' after-tax return increases with leverage.

While it is clear from these illustrations that leverage can increase the investors' return on equity, it is not always realized that their exposure to risk is also dramatically increased. Leverage is a double-edged sword that can magnify both profits and losses.

Figure 2.1
Comparison of Impact of Leverage
on Return on Equity (ROE)

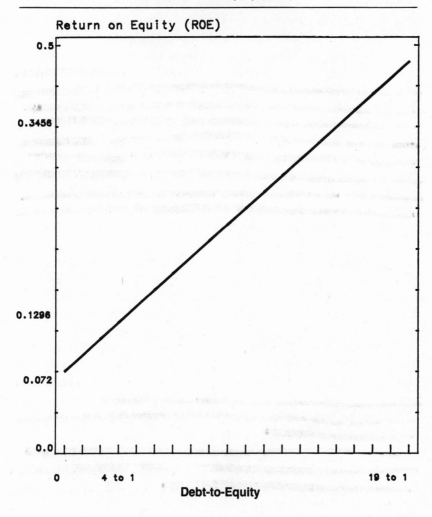

In fact, a simultaneous reduction in the return on an investment coupled with an increase in the cost of borrowed funds could be devastating. Individuals who borrowed to leverage their investment in oil and gas limited partnerships a few years ago saw the value of a barrel of crude oil plunge while the cost of their borrowed funds tied to the prime interest rate soared to rates of over 20 percent. Thus investors were faced with increasing interest payments and fewer dollars available from oil sales to cover their debt obligations.

Zero-Coupon Debt As a result of the passage of the Tax Reform Act of 1986, an increasing number of income-oriented limited partnerships are being structured so that investors receive sizable cash-free distributions in the early years. Often, these deals involve the use of zero-coupon debt instruments, which allows the partnership to distribute more cash to individual investors in the early years. At the due date, both the accrued interest and the original principal are paid to the lender. This requires a sizable cash drain on the partnership when the debt is paid and increases the investor's risk.

In these cases, investors must determine whether the appreciation of the partnership's assets will be sufficient to allow for the refinancing of the debt. In the event that the sponsors plan to terminate the partnership at the time the debt is due, investors must ascertain whether the proceeds are sufficient to pay off the debt, as well as their tax liability, and still provide them with an acceptable after-tax return.

Recourse and Nonrecourse Financing In addition to the liens placed directly on the properties to be financed, lenders often require borrowers to be personally liable. Recourse financing simply means that in the event that a note is in default, the lender can secure the delinquent payments from the borrowers directly.

Nonrecourse financing requires no personal backing, and the lender has no recourse if the obligations are not satisfied by the properties pledged as collateral. In this instance the borrower would not be required to personally guarantee the loan. The lender's risk may be greater under nonrecourse financing, and the borrower may therefore be required to pay a higher rate of interest.

Investment Interest Expense Limitation The amount of investment interest expense that taxpayers can deduct is limited to their net investment income. Net investment income equals gross investment income less investment expense.

SUMMARY

An understanding of the revenue and expense characteristics will aid potential investors in evaluating the relative attractiveness of an income-oriented limited partnership as compared to other competing investment choices. A *favorable after-tax return* is the result of the partnership's revenues exceeding its cash and noncash expenses during a given accounting year. These expenses can be comprised of organizational, management and development, operating, and financial costs.

Leverage, the use of debt financing in place of equity, enables individuals to write off more than the amount of cash investment. The desired effect of leveraging an investment is to increase the return on an individual's invested capital (*equity*) through the use of borrowed funds. The result of this use of debt is that investors experience a return on their invested capital far greater than the return on the project itself. The amount of debt invested relative to equity will be directly related to the return and risk experienced by investors.

In regard to the use of debt, taxpayers may be limited to the amount they can deduct. First, taxpayers are limited to the amount of investment interest expense they can deduct in any given year. Second, taxpayers are only allowed to deduct losses up to the amount for which they are at risk.

Chapter 3

Evaluating Income And Cash Flow Statements

A proper evaluation of limited partnerships requires that investors have a thorough understanding of the investment's financial statements. The two most important statements, the income statement and the cash flow statement are examined in depth in this chapter.

INCOME STATEMENTS

The income statement of a partnership for accounting or tax purposes reports the results of operations over a given period. This statement compares the revenues of a partnership with its expenses. If revenues exceed expenses, the partnership shows a profit. On the other hand, if expenses exceed revenues, the partnership shows a loss for the period.

In the early years, a partnership's income statement may report low profits. At first glance, this comparison of the partnership's revenues and expenses may seem misleading. However, a closer inspection might well reveal that some of the expenses resulting in low profits are noncash in nature. These items represent accounting charges against expenditures made in the past that did not require current cash outlays.

Depreciation is an excellent example of such a noncash expense. As mentioned in chapter 2, taxpayers who purchase certain assets are permitted to charge off their costs over a prescribed period of time. This yearly charge, called *depreciation*, is a deduction that is the result of a prior purchase of an asset and thus involves no cash outlay at the time depreciation is taken. However, for tax purposes, it is a deductible item. This and other noncash items enable investors to show minimal profits on their tax return, while at the same time often benefiting from potential tax-free cash distributions.

Suppose, for example, that investors have the opportunity to purchase a piece of equipment costing $100,000 that represents five-year property under the Accelerated Cost Recovery System (ACRS). Thus they will be entitled to receive deductions equal to 20 percent of the cost of the equipment each year.

Suppose further that investors put up the entire $100,000 and that revenues from this investment are expected to be $40,000 per year and operating expenses are estimated to be $15,000 per year. Table 3.1 represents the investors' income statement for the first year of this investment.

Table 3.1
Income Statement
For the Year Ended 19X1

Revenue	$40,000
Less:	
Operating expenses	15,000
Depreciation expense	20,000
Profit	$ 5,000
Tax liability (28 %)	$ 1,400

Table 3.1 shows that their investment results in a $5,000 profit for the first year. Given the investors' marginal tax rate of 28 percent, their first year's tax liability would be $1,400 (the profit times the investors' marginal tax rate). Thus the investors' initial outlay of $100,000 exposes them to a tax liability of $1,400 in year one.

CASH FLOW STATEMENTS

To offset this tax liability, the investors' outlay provides them with a positive cash flow (as shown in table 3.2).

Table 3.2
Cash Flow Statement
Unleveraged
For the Year Ended 19X1

Revenue	$40,000
Less:	
Operating expenses	15,000
Cash flow	$25,000

The investment would provide $25,000 in yearly cash flows over the first five years. The total annual return available to the investors would be $23,600, comprised of $25,000 of cash flow less $1,400 of tax liability.

The major advantage of the limited partnership form of business can be seen easily in this example. Even though this investment would provide the investors with a positive cash flow of $25,000, they are only taxed on the investment's "book" profits of $5,000 ($40,000 of revenue less the sum of $15,000 of cash operating expenses and $20,000 of depreciation). Thus, they receive $20,000 of additional cash without incurring any present tax liability. The investors' decision to purchase the equipment would hinge on the asset's expected after-tax cash flows over the investment period and its estimated residual value at the end of their planned holding period.

IMPACT OF DEBT

Now let's consider the impact of debt on the investors' first-year income and cash flow statements. Suppose that investors put up $50,000 and borrow the remainder or $50,000 over a ten-year period (assuming standard amortization) at an interest rate of eight percent per annum. Table 3.3 lists the interest, principal, debt service, and the remaining balance for each of the ten years that the investors' loan is in existence.

Table 3.3
Loan Amortization Schedule
$50,000
10-Year Loan at 8%

Year	Total interest	Total principal	Debt service	Remaining balance
1	$3,877.03	$3,402.65	$7,279.68	$46,597.35
2	3,594.62	3,685.06	7,279.68	42,912.30
3	3,288.74	3,990.94	7,279.68	38,921.36
4	2,957.52	4,322.16	7,279.68	34,599.20
5	2,598.75	4,680.93	7,279.68	29,918.26
6	2,210.27	5,069.41	7,279.68	24,848.85
7	1,789.48	5,490.20	7,279.68	19,358.65
8	1,333.80	5,945.88	7,279.68	13,412.77
9	840.30	6,439.38	7,279.68	6,973.39
10	305.85	6,973.39	7,279.24	0

As shown in table 3.3, the investors' debt service requirement will be $7,279 during each of the next ten years. In the initial, year more than half of the debt service requirement is composed of interest expenses totaling $3,887.03, while the retirement of principal is $3,402.65. As time passes, however, the amount of interest relative to the principal payments diminishes. Although the cash requirements remain constant over the ten-year loan, the tax deductions (interest expense) decrease over the life of the loan (see figure 3.1).

Figure 3.1
Debt Amortization

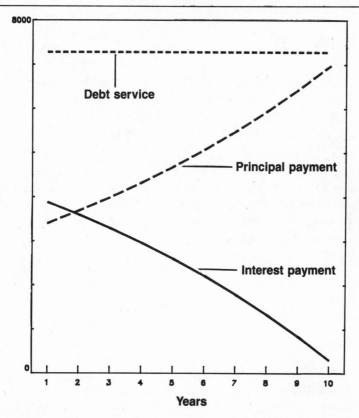

How will the investors' borrowing of $50,000 over a ten-year term affect their income statement and cash flow statement? (See the revised income statement in table 3.4).

Table 3.4
Revised Income Statement
For the Year Ended 19X1

Revenue	$40,000
Less:	
Operating expenses	15,000
Interest expense	3,877
Depreciation expense	20,000
Profit	$ 1,123
Tax liability (28%)	$ 314

Table 3.4 demonstrates that the investors' leveraged investment results in a taxable income of $1,123 for the first year. Given the investors' marginal tax rate of 28 per cent, their first-year tax liability would be approximately $314.44 ($1,123 X (1-0.28)). Thus, the investors' initial equity investment of $50,000 results in a first-year tax liability of $314.44.

In addition to the decreased first-year profits associated with borrowing, the investors' leveraged investment continues to provide them with a positive cash flow. The initial years' cash flow statement is shown in table 3.5.

Table 3.5
Cash Flow Statement (Leveraged)
For the Year Ended 19X1

Revenue	$40,000
Less:	
Operating expenses	15,000
Debt payment	7,280
Cash flow	$17,720

Thus, by utilizing leverage, the investors' total first year's return would now be $17,405.56, comprised of the $17,720 of cash flow less taxes due of $314.44. Their first years' return on equity would be 34.8 percent ($17,405.56/$50,000), versus 23.6 percent ($23,600/$100,000) under the unleveraged scenario.

Thus, in this instance, the investment becomes more attractive with the introduction of leverage. By borrowing $50,000, investors benefit from deducting interest charges, whereas they would have obtained fewer tax benefits without the additional benefit of leverage.

The immediate impact of leverage is quite clear in terms of its impact on taxable income and cash flow. What is not as clear is the investment's future prospects due to leverage. It is important to note that although the debt service requirements (dollar amount of payments) are constant, their composition is not. Specifically, deductible interest charges will fall over time, thus subjecting investors to greater tax exposure as more and more of the yearly debt servicing requirements are composed of principal repayments. Hence, interest deductions in subsequent years will likely decrease with the use of debt financing.

To illustrate this point, let's look at the net cash flow of the investment over a ten-year period. Assume that the revenues and expenses are the same (as found in tables 3.1 and 3.2) and that the amortization schedule is the same as the one in table 3.3.

In order to determine the net cash flows, we must first determine the investors' tax liability. Table 3.6 presents the income statements over the ten-year period. The last line of each year's income statement represents the investors' tax liability, which is found by multiplying the profit by their marginal tax rate. In this example, we assume a marginal tax rate of 28 percent.

As shown in table 3.6, the investors' tax liability gradually increases over the initial five-year period. This increase in exposure to taxes is a result of the lower interest expenses incurred as more principal has been paid off. In years six

Table 3.6
Income Statement
Investment Period

Year	1	2	3	4
Revenue	$40,000	$40,000	$40,000	$40,000
Less:				
Operating expenses	15,000	15,000	15,000	15,000
Interest expense	3,877	3,595	3,289	2,958
Depreciation expense	20,000	20,000	20,000	20,000
Profit	$ 1,123	$ 1,405	$ 1,711	$ 2,042
Tax liability (28%)	$ 314	$ 393	$ 479	$ 572

Year	5	6	7	8
Revenue	$40,000	$40,000	$40,000	$40,000
Less:				
Operating expenses	15,000	15,000	15,000	15,000
Interest expense	2,599	2,210	1,789	1,334
Depreciation expense	20,000	0	0	0
Profit	$ 2,401	$ 22,790	$23,211	$23,666
Tax liability (28%)	$ 672	$ 6,381	$ 6,499	$ 6,626

Year	9	10
Revenue	$40,000	$40,000
Less:		
Operating expenses	15,000	15,000
Interest expense	840	306
Depreciation expense	0	0
Profit	$24,160	$24,694
Tax liability (28%)	$ 6,765	$ 6,914

through ten, the investors' tax liability becomes even greater as the deduction for interest expense continues to drop and depreciation deductions are no longer available to help shield income.

The next step in determining the amount of yearly net cash flow is the development of cash flow statements. Since in this example the revenues, expenses, and debt servicing requirements remain constant, the cash flows for all ten years would be the same as in year one (see table 3.7 for the annual cash flow statement for the investment).

Table 3.7
Cash Flow Statement
(Investment Period)

Revenue	$40,000
Less:	
Operating expenses	15,000
Annual debt payment	7,280
Cash flow	$ 17,720

As shown in table 3.7, investors will experience annual cash flows of $17,720 during the initial ten-year period. However, as seen in table 3.6, investors will also be exposed to taxation on their income during this period. Table 3.8 reports the net cash flow to the investors over the ten-year period. Column (2) represents the investment's cash flow as calculated in table 3.7, while column (3) represents the investors' tax liability as calculated in table 3.6. Column (4) represents the investors' net cash flow and is found by subtracting their yearly tax liability (3), from their expected yearly cash flow (2).

The decision to purchase the equipment would depend not only on the investment's expected after-tax cash flows, but also on its likely residual. It should be noted, however, that under the leveraged alternative, the investors' initial cash investment is greatly reduced ($50,000 versus $100,000), as is their cash flow due to the servicing requirements of the debt.

Table 3.8
Calculation of Net Cash Flows

(1)	(2)	(3)	(4)
			(2) - (3)
			Net
	Cash	Tax	cash
Year	flow	liability	flow
1	$17,720	$ 314	$17,406
2	17,720	393	17,327
3	17,720	479	17,241
4	17,720	572	17,148
5	17,720	672	17,048
6	17,720	6,381	11,339
7	17,720	6,499	11,221
8	17,720	6,626	11,094
9	17,720	6,765	10,955
10	17,720	6,914	10,806

IMPACT OF INCREASING THE AMORTIZATION PERIOD

The relative proportion of interest and principal at any given time is determined by the length of the amortization and by the effective interest rate. The longer the term of the loan and the higher the interest rate, the greater the proportion of the initial interest charges to the total debt service requirement.

To understand this important concept, suppose that the loan in question was amortized over a 30-year period rather than the 10-year period used earlier. As shown in table 3.9, a sizable portion of the early years' debt servicing requirements is eaten up in interest charges, while little is left over to apply to the loan's principal. For example, in the first year only

Table 3.9
Loan Amortization Schedule
$50,000
30-Year Loan at 8 Percent

Year	Total interest	Total principal	Debt service	Remaining balance
1	$3,984.91	$ 417.65	$4,402.56	$49,582.35
2	3,950.24	452.32	4,402.56	49,130.04
3	3,912.69	489.87	4,402.56	48,640.18
4	3,872.04	530.52	4,402.56	48,109.66
5	3,827.99	574.57	4,402.56	47,539.09
6	3,780.31	622.25	4,402.56	46,912.84
7	3,728.67	673.89	4,402.56	46,238.95
8	3,672.75	729.81	4,402.56	45,509.14
9	3,612.15	790.41	4,402.56	44,718.73
10	3,546.56	856.00	4,402.56	43,862.73
11	3,475.50	927.06	4,402.56	42,935.66
12	3,398.58	1,003.98	4,402.56	41,931.68
13	3,315.23	1,087.33	4,402.56	40,844.35
14	3,225.00	1,177.56	4,402.56	39,666.79
15	3,127.25	1,275.31	4,402.56	38,391.48
16	3,021.41	1,381.15	4,402.56	37,010.33
17	2,906.79	1,495.77	4,402.56	35,514.57
18	2,782.62	1,619.94	4,402.56	33,894.63
19	2,648.16	1,754.40	4,402.56	32,140.23
20	2,502.56	1,900.00	4,402.56	30,240.23
21	2,344.86	2,057.70	4,402.56	28,182.53
22	2,174.06	2,228.50	4,402.56	25,954.03
23	1,989.10	2,413.46	4,402.56	23,540.57
24	1,788.80	2,613.76	4,402.56	20,926.81
25	1,571.84	2,830.72	4,402.56	18,096.09
26	1,336.91	3,065.65	4,402.56	15,030.44
27	1,082.45	3,320.11	4,402.56	11,710.33
28	806.88	3,595.68	4,402.56	8,114.65
29	508.44	3,894.12	4,402.56	4,220.53
30	185.23	4,220.53	4,402.56	0

$417.65 of the $4,402.56 in yearly debt service goes to principal reduction. Furthermore, interest charges exceed principal payments during the initial 21 years of the 30-year loan. These relationships can be observed graphically in figure 3.2.

Figure 3.2
Debt Amortization Schedule
30-Year Loan at 8 Percent

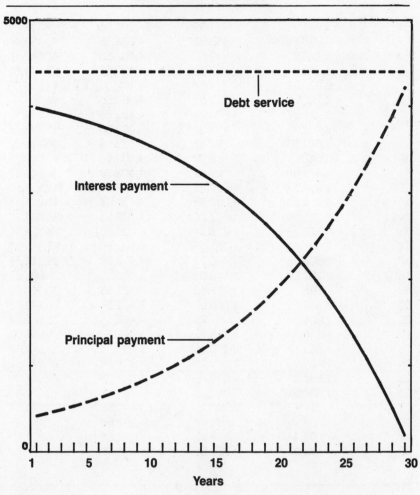

SUMMARY

As an investment, limited partnerships may possess tax advantages as well as economic value. Typically these investments experience low profits in the initial years. As such, they also have the ability to generate and distribute sizable amounts of cash tax-free. The ability to generate deductions while providing tax-free cash distributions is one of the key features of limited partnership investments.

Investors must know the difference between an investment's accounting profits and its cash flow characteristics in order to understand the mechanics of the limited partnership business form. The introduction of leverage allows investors to increase their after-tax returns while limiting their own invested capital. Investors must view the cash flow and tax effects over the life of the investment, since the use of debt as a tax shield will diminish over time.

Chapter 4

Evaluating Limited Partnership Performance Using Discounted Cash Flow Techniques

Most income-oriented limited partnership investments provide benefits that are received by the investors over several years. In addition, some investments require an individual to make equity contributions over a period of five years or longer. Since these contributions and corresponding benefits are spread out over time, investors must determine not only the actual cash flows of an investment but also the timing of these flows. While most of us who invest recognize that there is a time value of money, few of us incorporate the timing aspect of cash flows into our analysis of an investment.

Unfortunately, what investors often see in an offering memorandum is a schedule of yearly cash flows along with their cumulative value. Many times an investment's benefits seem very attractive; however, after carefully adjusting for the timing of these outflows and inflows, an investment may become marginal at best.

A restatement of cash inflows and outflows is needed as if they occurred at the same time. Once this is accomplished, investors can compare the value of their cash contributions (outflows) with the resulting inflows (cash distributions and net appreciation) in today's dollars.

TIME VALUE OF MONEY

There are numerous tools available to investors for measuring the impact of the time value of money on a particular investment opportunity. All of these revolve around the concepts embedded in the theory of compounding. The examples that follow demonstrate the principles of the time value of money.

Suppose investors are considering the purchase of a one-year certificate of deposit with an interest rate of ten percent per annum. If they deposit $10,000 with the bank for one year, what would their investment be worth at the end of the year? To answer this question, use the following formula:

Equation 4.1

$$FV = PV (1 + r)^n$$

where PV represents the present value of an investment (the investors' $10,000 investment in the bank CD) r represents the rate of interest in effect (ten percent), n represents the number of years the money is invested (one), and FV represents the future value of the investment (the value of the certificate of deposit at the end of one year).

Using the equation 4.1, we can calculate the future value of the investors' $10,000 initial investment over one year as follows:

$$FV = PV (1 + r)^n$$
$$FV = \$10,000(1.10)^1$$
$$FV = \$11,000$$

The investors' original investment of $10,000 invested at a rate of ten percent per annum will be worth $11,000 in one year. Thus we can readily determine the future value of an investment if we know the initial investment, the interest or compounding rate, and number of years the funds are invested. The interest or compounding rate, in effect, serves as an exchange rate through time, allowing investors to determine the future value based on their initial outlay.

For those who prefer not to use the formulas, appendix A (compound value of interest factor) can be used to solve the problem. Find the ten percent column and read down to year one to get the 1.100 factor needed.

Suppose that investors have the option of purchasing at the same rate a two-year certificate of deposit. What would their investment be worth at the end of two years? We can answer this question using equation 4.1. Applying this equation, we can calculate the future value of the investor's $10,000 initial investment at the end of the second year as follows:

$$FV = PV (1 + r)^n$$
$$FV = \$10,000 (1.10)^2$$
$$FV = \$10,000(1.210)$$
$$FV = \$12,100$$

Since the investment period is two years, n equals 2. The investors' original investment of $10,000 invested at a rate of ten percent per annum will be worth $12,100 in two years. Given an initial investment, the rate of interest, and the number of years, we can determine its future value. Appendix B represents the compound sum of an annuity factor which can be used for all annuities.

All of our examples have assumed yearly compounding. For more frequent compounding, simply divide the r term and multiply the n term in equation 4.1, by the number of times the interest is to be compounded per year. Hence, equation 4.2 for quarterly compounding is as follows:

Equation 4.2
$$FV = PV (1 + r / 4)^{n \cdot 4}$$

To illustrate this adjustment, let's suppose that the investor's $10,000 is invested at the same rate as before (ten percent) and for the same period (two years) but that it is compounded quarterly. Under these assumptions, we can determine the future value of the $10,000 initial investment at the end of the second year as follows:

$$FV = PV (1 + r / 4)^{n*4}$$
$$FV = \$10,000 (1 + 10 / 4)^{2*4}$$
$$FV = \$10,000(1.2184)$$
$$FV = \$12,184$$

Thus, original investment of $10,000 invested at an annual rate of ten percent compounded quarterly will be worth $12,184 in two years. The benefit of intrayear compounding can be seen by comparing the investment's terminal value under the yearly compounding scenario with its terminal value under the quarterly compounding scenario. Notice that quarterly compounding increases its terminal value by $84 over the terminal amount based on yearly compounding.

PRESENT VALUE ANALYSIS

We can use the same method with a slight modification to determine the present worth or value of expected future cash values. Therefore, if we know the future value of an investment (i.e., expected cash benefits), we can find the present value by adjusting the future investment through a *discount rate*, which represents an investor's required rate of return. We can develop the present value formula by rearranging our earlier future value formula by dividing both sides of the equation by $(1 + r)^n$. This is illustrated below:

Equation 4.3
$$PV = FV / (1 + r)^n$$

where PV represents the present value of an investment, r represents the appropriate discount rate, n represents the number of periods, and FV represents the future value of the investment.

In order to understand this technique, suppose that an investor is expecting to receive an inheritance of $20,000 at the end of one year. Assume that the investor's required rate of return during this period is expected to be eight percent. What is the value of the inheritance today? To answer this question, we need to know the future expected cash flow (the $20,000 inheritance) and the appropriate discount rate (eight percent). This can be calculated using the present value formula:

$$PV = FV / (1 + r)^n$$
$$PV = \$20{,}000/(1.08)^1$$
$$PV = \$18{,}520$$

Thus, the present value of the $20,000 inheritance to be received at the end of the year is worth $18,520 today, assuming a discount rate of eight percent. In other words, the $18,520 reflects the present value of the $20,000 inheritance to be received in one year. The eight percent acts as an exchange rate through time, allowing us to determine an investment's value today.

Dividing cash flows by $(1 + r)^n$ can be a rather cumbersome process. To avoid this problem, we can find the present value of an investment through the use of discount tables (such as those in appendices C and D) or any financial calculator. Using our present example, we reach the following:

$$PV = FV / (1 + r)^n$$
$$PV = \$20{,}000/(1.08)^1$$
$$PV = \$20{,}000 \text{ X } 0.92593$$
$$PV = \$18{,}519$$

The present value factor of a dollar to be received in one year at eight percent is 0.92593 (appendix C under one year at eight percent). The value 0.92593 was calculated by dividing $1 by $(1.08)^1$. Thus a dollar received in one year is equivalent to receiving $0.92593 today.

Assume that the investor will receive the inheritance in two years. We can determine its present worth, or *present value*, by multiplying the amount expected ($20,000) by the appropriate discount factor for two years at eight percent or 0.85734 (as found in appendix C). Thus the present value of the $20,000 inheritance due in two years would be $17,147.

Finally, assume that the investor is to receive the inheritance in a series of four equal yearly payments of $5,000 beginning at the end of next year. What would be the present value or worth of these future receipts? In order to answer this question, we could solve the following equation:

$PV = (\$5,000/(1.08)^1) + (\$5,000/(1.08)^2) +$
  $(\$5,000/(1.08)^3) + (\$5,000/(1.08)^4)$

$PV = \$4,630 + \$4,285 + \$3,970 + \$3,675$

$PV = \$16,560$

However, there is a much easier way of solving this problem. These cash flows represent an *annuity* (since they are equal in amount). The present value of an annuity can be determined by multiplying the yearly amount expected ($5,000) by the appropriate discount factor for four years at eight percent or 4.506 (as found in appendix D). Thus the present value of the $20,000 inheritance due in two years would be $16,560.

Actually the present value of a $1 annuity table found in appendix D represents the sum of the present value found in appendix C. Both tables give the same results, but in cases where annuities are involved appendix C produces results much more quickly.

DISCOUNTED CASH FLOW MODELS

The discounting techniques just discussed can be used to adjust an investment's cash flows so that they can be evaluated based on the concept of the time value of money. We present two of the more popular methods of discounting below.

Discounted cash flow techniques allow investors to review the profitability of a income-oriented limited partnership over its life. Specifically, discounted cash flow techniques compare investment outlays with their forecast cash inflows and tax benefits.

These approaches recognize that a dollar received today is more valuable than a dollar received tomorrow. Thus these approaches incorporate the time value of money into the decision-making process. Hence, discounted cash flows serve as an exchange rate mechanism whereby the values of net cash inflows (the excess of cash savings over cash expenditures- realized in future time periods are adjusted (discounted back) to reflect their present value, thus allowing an apple-to-apple basis of comparison.

The two most popular discounted cash flow models are net present value and internal rate of return. Each of these models are explained in detail below.

Net Present Value

The net present value method involves discounting the expected cash flows (cash distributions less tax liability) over the life of the investment at a required rate of return and then comparing the present value of these cash flows with the investment's required outlays.

If the present value of benefits exceeds the present value of required cash outlays, the investment is said to have a positive net present value (that is, present value of the cash inflows minus the present value of the cash outlays), and it would therefore be accepted. A positive net present value indicates that the actual return on the investment is greater than the rate required by the investor. However, if the investment's present value of cash outlays is greater than the present value of the cash inflows, it would be rejected since it fails to achieve the investor's minimum required rate of return.

Now we will illustrate the net present value (NPV) technique using our previous sample investment. The revenue was expected to be $40,000 and operating expenses were estimated to be $15,000 per year. Suppose further that the investment would represent a purchase of five-year property under ACRS and that investors would write off the cost of the investment ($100,000) evenly over the five-year period after which they would receive $10,000 (year six) for the investment net of taxes. (With the passage of the Tax Reform Act of 1986, taxpayers are required to use a revised Accelerated Cost Recovery System (ACRS) for assets placed in service after December 31, 1986. As explained in chapter 2, under this system the yearly depreciation deductions under the ACRS are determined by the asset's class life. The taxpayer adopts the appropriate write-off as dictated by it asset class. In the case of equipment, the revised ACRS provides for accelerated depreciation with a crossover to the straight-line method with the half-year convention.)

Thus, taxpayers would only be allowed to take a depreciation deduction of $20,000 per year. Their yearly tax liability can be calculated by using table 4.1.

Table 4.1
Investment's Tax Liability
(28 Percent Tax Bracket)

Year	Revenue	Operating expenses	Depreciation	Taxable income	Tax liability
1	$40,000	$15,000	$20,000	$5,000	$ 1,400
2	40,000	15,000	20,000	5,000	1,400
3	40,000	15,000	20,000	5,000	1,400
4	40,000	15,000	20,000	5,000	1,400
5	40,000	15,000	20,000	5,000	1,400

The taxable income column represents revenue minus the sum of operating expenses and depreciation. The tax liability column represents the product of taxable income and the investors' marginal tax rate of 28 percent. As we mentioned earlier, the higher the marginal tax rate, the greater the tax liability.

Individuals with marginal tax rates other than 28 percent can substitute their rate into the equation. For example, an individual contemplating the same investment as the investor just discussed but who is in the 15 percent tax bracket would receive tax benefits such as those indicated in table 4.2.

Table 4.2
Investment's Tax Liability
15 Percent Tax Bracket

Year	Revenue	Operating expenses	Depreciation	Taxable income	Tax liability
1	$40,000	$15,000	$20,000	$5,000	$ 750
2	40,000	15,000	20,000	5,000	750
3	40,000	15,000	20,000	5,000	750
4	40,000	15,000	20,000	5,000	750
5	40,000	15,000	20,000	5,000	750

An individual who is in the 15 percent tax bracket has only half the tax liability of the investor in the 28 percent bracket, despite the fact that both are making the same investment. This is because of the impact of marginal tax rates (discussed in chapter 1).

To obtain the total cash effect from the investment, we must subtract the yearly tax liability amount from the corresponding yearly cash flow amount. Column 2 of table 4.3 represents the yearly tax liability for an investor in the 28 percent tax bracket (see table 4.1), while column 3 represents the expected yearly cash distribution of the investment ($50,000 of revenue less $15,000 of cash operating expenses); column 4 is found by subtracting column 2 from column 3.

Table 4.3
Summary of Investment Returns
(28 Percent Tax Bracket)

Year	Tax liability	Cash distribution		Net cash distribution
1	$1,400	$25,000		$23,600
2	1,400	25,000		23,600
3	1,400	25,000		23,600
4	1,400	25,000		23,600
5	1,400	25,000		23,600
6	0	10,000	(Proceeds)	10,000

Under the net present value approach, the next step is to apply a discount rate to the yearly net cash distribution column appearing in table 4.3 in order to determine the present value of the investor's cash distributions less any tax liabilities. The discount rate chosen should correspond to an individual's required rate of return. (For illustration purposes we will use a discount rate of ten percent.) The formula for this operation using the cash flows in table 4.3 is as follows:

$$\text{NPV} = + (\$23,600/(1.1)^1) + (\$23,600/(1.1)^2)$$
$$+ (\$23,600/(1.1)^3) + (\$23,600/(1.1)^4)$$
$$+ (\$23,600/(1.1)^5) + (10,000/(1.1)^6) - 100,000$$

$$\text{NPV} = -\$4,898$$

Fortunately, discount tables (such as those provided in appendices A-D) are available to ease the difficulty of working with cumbersome formulas. This method allows for ease of calculation and is demonstrated here. The present value of the inflows is found by multiplying the net cash distributions column by their corresponding discount factors obtained from appendix C. Using the ten-percent discount factor, the net cash distribution in table 4.3 yields the following results shown in table 4.4.

Table 4.4
Total Tax Benefit and Cash Distributions
Using a 10-percent Discount Factor
(Straight-Line Depreciation)

Year	Net cash distribution	Discount factor	Present value
1	$ 23,600	0.90909	$21,363
2	23,600	0.82645	19,504
3	23,600	0.75131	17,731
4	23,600	0.68301	16,119
5	23,600	0.62092	14,654
6	10,000	0.56400	5,640
Total	$128,000		$95,102

At first glance, the investment described in table 4.4 might appear to be attractive, since an investment of $100,000 provided total benefits of $128,000 over the investment's life. However, the simple summing of net cash distributions ignores the fact that these amounts are spread throughout time and thus do not reflect the true value of the investment measured in today's dollars.

It is necessary to adjust these amounts to reflect the timing of their occurrence. The net present value approach allows us to do this. Using the data from table 4.4, we can calculate the present value to be $95,102. Since the investor's initial outlay was $100,000, we simply reduce the present value of the inflows by this amount. The result is that the net present value of the investment is -$4,898.

From the net present value standpoint, the investment would be rejected,since it would provide a return less than the ten percent specified. It should be pointed out that the net present value method does not measure the actual percentage of the rate of return on the investment but merely determines whether the investment's return is greater or less than the return required.

Internal Rate of Return

The internal rate of return (IRR) model requires investors to calculate the rate of return of an investment by solving for the discount factor that causes the present value of the cash flow stream to equal its initial outlay. Again, by using our earlier example, we can calculate the IRR as follows:

$$\text{Equation 4.4}$$
$$\text{PVCI} - \text{IO} = 0$$

where PVCI represents the present value of cash inflows discounted at the IRR, and IO represents the investment's initial outlay. With our present example, the equation is as follows:

$$\text{IRR} = (23,600/(1 + r)^1) + (23,600/(1 + r)^2) + (23,600/(1 + r)^3) + (23,600/(1 + r)^4) + (23,600/(1 + r)^5) + (10,000/(1 + r)^6) - 100,000 = 0$$

$$r = \text{IRR} = 8.19\%$$

In this instance the IRR is approximately 8.2 percent. This confirms our earlier results using the NPV approach, which indicated that the expected return is less than the rate of return demanded (ten percent).

SELECTING THE REQUIRED RATE OF RETURN

The importance of selecting the correct discount rate can be readily seen in the above example. Had the investors required an after-tax rate of return of 8 percent (rather than 10 percent) the investment would be acceptable. Thus, the required rate of return is the cornerstone of discounted cash flow analysis.

There is an inverse relationship between the discount rate and the net present value of an investment. Hence, applying a higher discount rate to a future cash flow series will cause the present value of that cash flow series to decrease. This relationship can be viewed graphically in figure 4-1.

Figure 4.1
Present Value and Discount Rate

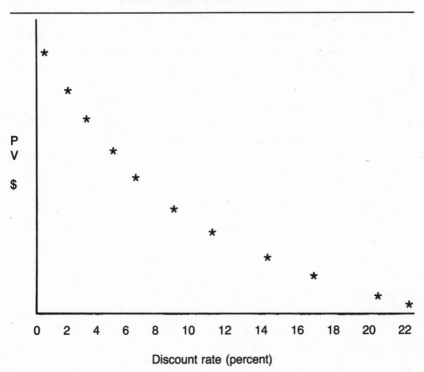

The investors' required rate of return is a function of the time value of money and investment risk. Obviously, investors who choose to invest their money for a given period of time would at the very least want to receive a return in order to maintain its same purchasing power when the funds are returned to them.

In addition to receiving a return equal to the time value of money, investors should demand an additional return based on the risk of the investment itself. Investment risk will vary from one investment to another. The major categories of investment risk are business risk, market risk, and liquidity risk.

Business risk refers to the limited partnership's ability to remain profitable. In assessing a business risk, the investor must evaluate the holdings of the limited partnership in terms of current economic conditions in order to determine its continued success. In addition, a detailed evaluation of the partnership's management, including its track record and experience, is essential to the analysis of its business risk.

In addition to business risk, the master limited partnership investor may also be exposed to market risk. Market risk refers to the risk of a drop in the market price of the master limited partnership security due to changes in the stock market itself. Many stock prices tend to be positively correlated with the market. Thus, shifts in stock prices may be largely independent of the company's operating performance. The investor must therefore identify the securities' responsiveness to the market.

Limited partnership units are considered to be extremely illiquid investments. Unlike master limited partnerships, where active secondary markets exist, the typical limited partnership must be held for a indeterminable period of time. In these instances, the investor should demand a premium due to the investment's lack of liquidity.

SUMMARY

The proper evaluation of a income-oriented limited partnership investment requires the adjustment of future cash inflows through discounting techniques so that their present worth can be compared with the capital contributions of the investor. Among the various techniques available are net present value and internal rate of return.

Under the *net present value method*, cash inflows are discounted to reflect the timing of their occurrence and their overall riskiness. The present value of inflows are then compared with the initial outlay to determine if the project provides a minimum acceptable return. If the net present value is positive, an investor accepts the project; if the net present value is negative, an investor rejects it. The discount rate (or hurdle rate) must reflect not only the impact of inflation but also the risk level of the investment.

The *internal rate of return method* allows investors to calculate the true rate of return on an investment by solving for the discount rate that causes the present value of the inflows to equal the cash outlay. This return is then compared with investors' required return to determine the investment's attractiveness.

Chapter 5

Evaluating Limited Partnerships' Financial Statements Using Breakeven Analysis

Sponsors of limited partnership interests will usually provide investors with detailed *pro forma* (forecast) financial statements, using assumptions that will reflect a best-case scenario. Accompanying these statements will be the usual disclaimers, indicating that the future is unknown and that the *pro forma* statements must be read with that in mind.

Investors must judge how well these assumptions are likely to hold. Additionally, they should try to determine when what appears to be a good deal on paper will turn bad. They must be aware of the sensitivity of an investment to the assumptions underlying the sponsor's analysis. Along these lines, investors must determine the level of revenues and expenses necessary to ensure an investment's success.

One method of evaluating the revenue capabilities of an investment is breakeven analysis. Under this method, the characteristics of both revenue and expenses are examined to identify the investment's *breakeven point*, or the amount of revenue needed to cover all expenses. A comparison of breakeven sales with forecast sales levels will give insight into the investment's risks.

The starting point in the development of breakeven analysis is the separation of the investment's costs into its variable and fixed components. A *variable cost* is one that is expected to change directly with output or production. Thus, as revenues increase or decrease, variable costs will increase or decrease proportionately.

An example of a variable cost in a production operation would be operating expenses, such as material costs, which are directly related to sales. As sales and production increase, material requirements would also be expected to rise. If production ceases, then no material costs would be incurred. In the typical limited partnership, many of the general partners' fees will also be variable in nature. For example, the leasing and management fees are variable costs, since they are stated as a percentage of the project's yearly revenues.

A *fixed cost*, on the other hand, will remain the same, regardless of the level of output. Costs such as the organizational expenses (described in chapter 2) would fall into the category of fixed cost. Similarly, depreciation expenses would normally be fixed in nature. Another example of a fixed cost is property taxes, since they are levied based on the value of the property (and thus would not vary with output or sales).

DOLLAR SALES AND BREAKEVEN ANALYSIS

The dollar sales breakeven point can be calculated using the following formula:

$$\text{Breakeven point} = \frac{FC}{\frac{TR-VC}{TR}}$$

where TR represents total revenue, VC represents variable costs, and FC represents fixed costs.

The ratio of revenue minus variable costs divided by revenue is commonly referred to as the percentage of marginal contribution (MC%). The resulting breakeven point indicates the level of revenue necessary to cover total costs (variable and fixed costs).

To illustrate these calculations, let's reexamine the previous chapter's $100,000 investment (unleveraged). Remember that revenue was expected to be $40,000 and that operating expense was assumed to be $15,000. Further assume that of this total, variable costs equal 25 percent of sales ($10,000), and that fixed costs other than depreciation and debt servicing requirements are $5,000. In addition, the investment will provide depreciation in year one of $20,000. Therefore, in this example, total fixed costs in this example will equal $25,000 ($5,000 operating fixed costs and $20,000 depreciation expenses).

BEP = $25,000 / (($40,000 - $10,000) / $40,000)
BEP = $25,000/(0.75)
BEP = $33,333

The investment must generate sales of $33,333 in order to break even (to cover both its variable and fixed costs). Every dollar of sales beyond the breakeven point ($33,333) will increase profits by $0.75.

The relationship between revenue, total cost (variable and fixed cost), and the investment's breakeven point is depicted graphically in figure 5.1. The breakeven sales level is represented on the graph at the point where the total revenue line intersects the total cost line (variable and fixed costs). At this point, total revenue equals total costs, and total profits (and total losses) would be zero.

Figure 5.1
Breakeven Analysis

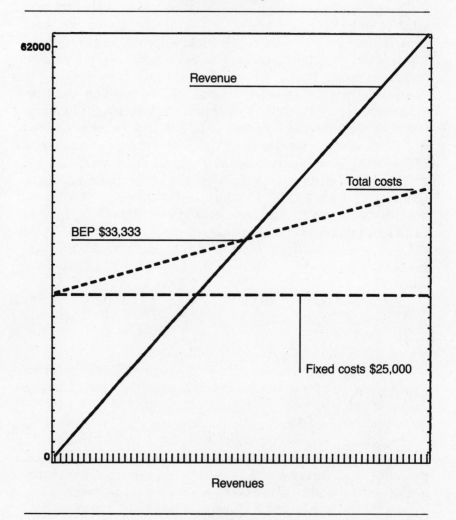

Revenue

Total costs

62000

BEP $33,333

Fixed costs $25,000

0

Revenues

Breakeven analysis can also be demonstrated using an income statement format (see table 5.1).

Table 5.1
Breakeven Analysis
(Income Statement)
For the Year Ended 19X1

Revenue	$33,333
Less operating expenses:	
Variable costs (25% of revenue)	8,333
Fixed costs	5,000
Depreciation expense	20,000
Profit (loss)	$0

Table 5.1 demonstrates that the breakeven point is indeed $33,333 in revenue. Thus the investment will show a loss in the first year as long as total revenue is less than $33,333. If revenue is greater than this amount, the project will show a profit.

CASH BREAKEVEN ANALYSIS

Although the $33,333 of revenue is at the breakeven point, it will still generate a positive cash flow—since fixed costs include depreciation, which is a noncash expense. We can modify the formula to solve for the *cash breakeven point* by eliminating the dollar amount of depreciation from our fixed costs totals. The cash breakeven point (Cash BEP) is calculated as follows:

$$\text{Cash breakeven point} = \frac{\text{Cash FC}}{\frac{\text{TR-VC}}{\text{TR}}}$$

Cash BEP = $5,000 / (($40,000 - $10,000) / $40,000)
Cash BEP = $5,000/(0.75)
Cash BEP = $6,667

Thus, the cash breakeven point will be $6,667 (see table 5.2).

Table 5.2
Breakeven Analysis
(Income Statement)
For the Year Ended 19X1

Revenue	$6,667
Less operating expenses:	
Variable costs (25% of revenue)	1,667
Cash fixed costs	5,000
Cash flow	0

A comparison of the revenue required using our first breakeven-point formula and the revenue required using the cash breakeven-point formula is quite revealing. The revenue required to cover all cash and noncash expenses is five times as great as the revenue necessary to cover the cash expenses. This comparison indicates that while $33,333 is needed before the investment shows a profit, only $6,667 of revenue is needed to cover cash expenses. Hence, levels of revenue between the cash breakeven point of $6,667 and the sales breakeven point of $33,333 will provide the investor with a positive cash flow even though the investment will show a loss.

BREAKEVEN ANALYSIS AND LEVERAGE

The introduction of financial leverage requires modification of the breakeven-point formula. In addition to usual operating

expenses the model must take into account both the impact of
interest expense and the repayment of principal. Both of these
items represent fixed charges in the sense that they are not
expected to vary with output.

Interest expense, which is a fixed cost, can simply be added
to the existing level of fixed costs. Hence, while interest expenses are paid from before-tax earnings and thus are deductible items, the repayment of debt principal must be made from
after-tax earnings. This requires an adjustment of the repayment of principal to reflect its before-tax service requirements.

The leverage breakeven-point formula enables investors to
calculate the level of revenue needed not only to cover fixed
operating expenses, but also to provide funds for debt servicing requirements. The dollar sales breakeven point adjusted
for leverage can be calculated using the following formula:

$$\text{Breakeven point} = \frac{FC + \dfrac{\text{Principal}}{1\text{-MTR}}}{\dfrac{\text{TR-VC}}{\text{TR}}}$$

Where MTR represents the investors' marginal tax rate

In this instance, we modify our earlier model by increasing
fixed costs by the annual interest charges, plus the dollar
amount of before-tax funds needed to cover the loan's principal repayment. The total dollars required before tax will be
related to the amount of the principal payment and the investors' marginal tax rate.

To illustrate the application of the leveraged breakeven
point formula, let us again use our current investment example. Remember that the investors borrowed $50,000 to finance
the investment over a ten-year period at an interest rate of
eight percent per annum with annual debt servicing requirements of $7,280 ($3,877 in interest expense and $3,403 in

. principal repayment the first year). Using this and information provided earlier, we can calculate the initial year's leveraged breakeven point:

BEP = $\dfrac{(\$28,877 + (\$3,403/(1 - 0.28)))}{(\$40,000 - \$10,000)/\$40,000}$

BEP = $(\$28,877 + \$4,726)/(0.75)$

BEP = $\$33,603/(0.75)$

BEP = $\$44,804$

This analysis reveals that the investment must generate revenues of $44,804 to cover variable costs and fixed costs (including interest charges and required principal repayment). Each dollar of revenue above this level ($44,804) will again increase profits by $0.75. This relationship is shown graphically in figure 5.2.

Figure 5.2
Breakeven Analysis

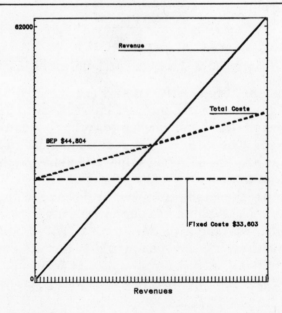

In this example, the use of borrowed funds by the investor increases the breakeven point from $33,333 to $44,804. Thus, we can see that the use of leverage does in fact increase the riskiness of the investment. Where before the investor needed $33,333 to break even, the additional fixed cost associated with the use of debt will require a sales increase of 34.4 percent to cover all costs. Hence, with the potential of additional reward comes the acceptance of additional risk.

As depicted in figure 5.2, the breakeven point is where the total revenue line intersects the total cost line (variable and fixed costs). In this example, fixed costs include fixed operating expenses, interest expense, and the amount needed before tax to service the yearly principal payment. At this point, total revenue equals total costs; therefore, the total profits (after debt servicing) would be zero.

The breakeven analysis can again be demonstrated using the income statement format by incorporating the debt servicing requirements into the analysis (see table 5.3).

Table 5.3
Breakeven Analysis
(Income Statement)
For the Year Ended 19X1

Revenue	$44,804
Less operating expenses:	
Variable costs (25% of revenue)	11,201
Fixed costs	5,000
Interest expense	3,877
Depreciation expense	20,000
Profits before taxes and principal payment	4,726
Less:	
Tax liability (28% of profit)	1,323
Funds for principal repayment	$ 3,403

Table 5.3 confirms that the breakeven point is $44,804 in revenue. Remember that the investment will still have positive cash flow after debt servicing, since depreciation, a non-cash expense, amounts to $20,000 in the initial year.

CASH BREAKEVEN POINT AND LEVERAGE

As demonstrated in our unleveraged example, we can modify the formula to solve for the cash breakeven point, by subtracting depreciation from our fixed costs. The cash breakeven point then would be calculated as follows:

$$\text{Cash BEP} = \frac{\text{CFC} + \left(\dfrac{\text{Principal}}{1\text{-MTR}}\right)}{\left(\dfrac{\text{TR-VC}}{\text{TR}}\right)}$$

$$\text{Cash BEP} = \frac{(8{,}877 + (\$3{,}403/(1 - 0.28))}{(\$40{,}000 - \$10{,}000)/\$40{,}000}$$

Cash BEP = ($8,877 + $4,726)/(0.75)

Cash BEP = $13,603 / (0.75)

Cash BEP = $18,137

Thus, the cash breakeven point (leveraged) or the revenue needed to cover all costs (including debt servicing requirements) is $18,137. Table 5.4 illustrates the cash breakeven point utilizing the income statement format.

Table 5.4
Breakeven Analysis
(Income Statement)
For the Year Ended 19X1

Revenue	$18,137
Less operating expenses:	
Variable costs (25% of revenue)	4,534
Fixed costs	5,000
Interest expense	3,877
Profits before taxes and principal payment	4,726
Less:	
Tax liability (28% of profit)	1,323
Funds for principal repayment	$ 3,403

As depicted in table 5.4, the breakeven revenue of $18,137 is sufficient to cover all fixed and variable costs while providing the investor with taxable income of $4,726. Given the investor's marginal tax rate of 28 percent, the investor will incur $1,323 in taxes (taxable income of $4,726 times the marginal tax rate of 28 percent) and be left with the $3,403 necessary to cover principal repayment requirements.

SUMMARY

This analysis enables investors to compare forecast revenues with those necessary to break even or cover all costs. A comparison of the two will provide insight about the riskiness of an investment. This approach can be adapted to consider leveraged investments in which it is necessary to cover not only operating costs but also debt servicing requirements.

A proper assessment of the desirability of a particular investment can be determined through the use of breakeven analysis, which pinpoints the level of sales necessary for the investment to break even, in terms of profit generation. This tool can also be adapted to focus on the cash requirements of an investment. Further modifications can allow investors to study the impact of debt financing on the profits and cash requirements of the investment.

Chapter 6

How To Screen Limited Partnerships Using An Offering Memorandum

Limited partnership interests in income-oriented investments are usually marketed through the use of a prospectus or an offering memorandum. Sponsors of public offerings are required to provide investors with a prospectus. While sponsors of private offerings are not required to provide potential investors with such a document, they usually will provide investors with an offering memorandum containing much of the same information contained in a prospectus. The sponsors of these offerings are required to provide the investor with all relevant information needed to arrive at a sound investment decision. An understanding of the origin of the disclosure requirements will provide insight into the role that various government bodies play in this process.

We will first present a brief overview of this process and examine the roles of both the federal and state governments in the regulation of securities offerings. Then we'll turn our attention to the contents of these documents.

Chapter 6

FEDERAL ROLE IN THE REGULATION OF SECURITIES

Securities offerings are regulated at the federal and/or state levels. The Securities Act of 1933 was enacted by the federal government to regulate securities dealings. In 1934, Congress passed the Securities and Exchange Act, which created the Securities and Exchange Commission (SEC), the organization responsible for the administration of these laws.

The Securities and Exchange Act of 1933 requires full disclosure on the part of the issuer in the form of a prospectus at the time of a public offering. The prospectus must contain all pertinent information needed to make an intelligent decision and must be filed with the SEC before its offering to the public.

Subsequent approval by the SEC simply means that the prospectus is in compliance with the 1933 act. The SEC does not pass judgment on the correctness of its contents. It merely indicates that the prospectus complies with the act. Every prospectus must display the following on its first page: "These securities have not been approved or disapproved by the Securities and Exchange Commission, nor has the Commission passed upon the accuracy of this prospectus. Any representation to the contrary is a criminal offense."

For its approval of a public offering of limited partnership units, the SEC's only concern is with the disclosure requirements, not with the merits of the investment. Thus registration with the SEC should not be viewed as an attribute of the deal.

EXEMPT SECURITIES

Unlike public offerings, certain securities offerings are exempt from SEC registration. For example, intrastate offerings may be exempt from registration. Additionally, exemptions from registration at the federal level are granted for "limited" or "private" placements. Limited offerings are exempt from SEC registration because of their relative small size and the heavy burden placed on them by complying with the costly registration requirements.[1] Private offerings are exempt because of the personal relationship between the issuer and purchaser of the securities.[2]

Sponsors of limited and/or private offerings must provide investors with a private placement or offering memorandum at the start of the selling effort. Although these documents may contain much of the information required in a prospectus, the avoidance of the time-consuming registration process cuts red tape and provides a more efficient environment for capital formation. While the sponsors are still required to file with the SEC, the paperwork involved in limited or private offerings is much less than would be required under the normal registration process.

Exemption from the federal registration requirement may be accomplished through either regulation A or regulation D. Regulation A provides for exemption from registration of limited offerings under $1,500,000. Exemption under regulation A is chiefly for stock offerings and is seldom used for tax shelters. The purpose of this exemption (regulation A) is to free the smaller offerings from the costly compliance provisions of the registration process. Thus it was felt that these registration requirements placed an undue burden on the smaller issues. [3]

Regulation A was intended to provide an inexpensive alternative to securities registration. However, the complexities of

1 Sargent, Mark A., "State Limited and Private Offering Exemptions: The Maryland Experience in a National Perspective" *University of Baltimore Law Review.* 13:3 (Spring 1984), p. 497.

2 Sargent, p. 497.

3 Sargent, p. 506.

compliance to regulation A has proved costly in many instances and thus limited its usefulness for income-oriented limited partnerships.

The introduction of regulation D has provided syndicators with several options for seeking exemption from the costly SEC registration process. Regulation D permits exemption on issues up to an aggregate offering price of $500,000 under its rule 504 and $5,000,000 under rule 505 of regulation D, assuming all other requirements are met.[4] Furthermore, under rule 506 of regulation D there is no aggregate dollar offering limitation.[5]

In general, the rules associated with meeting the exemption requirements under regulation D concern themselves with the nature and number of purchasers of the securities offered. Regulation D permits the partnership to offer an unlimited number of "accredited investors" as defined in its rule 215, while limiting the number of nonaccredited investors (rule 506 of regulation D) to a maximum of 35 who are otherwise deemed suitable at the discretion of the sponsors.[6]

Certain organizations may be qualified under the accredited investor provisions of regulation D. In addition, those individuals who meet one of the following requirements are deemed to be accredited investors and as such are not counted in arriving at the participation limit:

1. A net worth (individual or joint) in excess of $1,000,000 at purchase date.
2. Individual gross income in excess of $200,000 in each of the last two years and an expected income in excess of $200,000 again in the year of purchase.
3. Purchases over $150,000 in securities, in which the total purchase price is less than five times the individual's net worth.

4 Sargent, p. 509.
5 Sargent, p. 509.
6 Sargent, p. 509.

To comply with the exemption requirements of regulation D, sponsors must limit their offerings in two ways: (1) investors must meet the accredited investors' requirements, and (2) there must be no more than 35 nonaccredited but otherwise suitable investors.

STATE SECURITIES LAWS

Exemption at the federal level does not imply that the securities are exempt from registration at the state level. In addition to compliance with federal regulations, sponsors may also be compelled to meet the requirements of the states in which their securities are offered for sale.

Important differences exist in terms of the intent of legislation at the federal and state levels. The SEC is chiefly concerned with full and complete disclosure of information to investors in a timely manner. In addition to the full disclosure requirement, many state laws require an offering to meet certain fairness tests designed to protect potential investors from overexposure to risk and promotion abuses.[7]

Due to the fairness or "merit" requirement imposed at the this level, exemptions may be more difficult to obtain in some states than in other states or at the federal level. Sponsors may elect to seek exemption at the state level by complying with the state's exemption requirements, or they simply may not offer the units for sale in those states where compliance is too costly or difficult. Meeting the SEC exemption requirements does not guarantee compliance at the state level.

State security statutes, called "blue sky laws," were enacted over the years to protect investors from fraud and deception. The first such law was enacted in Kansas. At first, the content

7 Makens, Hugh H., "Who Speaks for the Investor? An Evaluation of the Assault on Merit Regulation." *University of Baltimore Law Review.* 13:3 (Spring 1984), p. 436.

of these state securities laws varied widely from state to state. Most blue sky laws have since been rewritten and are now patterned after the Uniform Securities Act. Differences do still exist, although not to the extent that they once did.

CONTENTS OF AN OFFERING MEMORANDUM

Reading an offering memorandum or a prospectus can be a time-consuming task. Lengthy and full of legal jargon, these rather intimidating documents can be several hundred pages long. While screening favorable income-oriented limited partnership investments through a prospectus or offering memorandum might seem an impossible task, it can be done in a few hours.

The reason for this is simple: Certain areas of the offering memorandum are of a generic nature; they can be found in most limited partnerships of the kind you are evaluating. Usually, an offering memorandum or prospectus will contain about 75 percent "boiler plate" information, which is common to most limited partnership investments of the kind being examined.

The secret is knowing where not to look. After you develop an understanding of these generic sections, you can avoid spending time needlessly reviewing these areas. You can direct your attention to the remaining 25 percent of the offering memorandum, which deals with the investment itself. This will enable you to spend your time focusing on the critical aspects of the investment.

These documents are usually divided into the following areas: estimated use of proceeds, investment objectives and policies, project description, sources of invested capital, partnership allocations, compensation to general partners, management history and prior records, pro forma estimates, project risks, tax aspects, agreement of limited partnership, suitability standards, and the subscription documents. We describe each of these parts of an offering memorandum or prospectus in the sections that follow, highlighting the information to be found in each part of the disclosure document as well as indicating the areas that require your scrutiny.

UNIQUE OFFERING MEMORANDUM ELEMENTS

We will begin by describing the sections (25 percent) that relate to the limited partnership itself. You should devote your time to fully understanding these sections first.

Estimated Use of Proceeds

The estimated use of proceeds statement can be quite revealing. In effect, this statement shows how the capital raised is going to be used. By inspecting this statement, investors can determine how much of theirmoney is actually going into the project and how much is going into the sponsor's pocket or otherwise being eaten up in fees.

Investors should determine what percentage of the capital being raised is allocated to such front-end fees. Reasonable fees associated with organizing the limited partnership, marketing the units, and for other legal and accounting items are to be expected. As a general rule, investors should shy away from investments in which over 15 percent of the total capital is allocated to fees. The higher this percentage, the more of your money will end up in the sponsor's pocket.

Investment Objectives and Policies

The statement of objectives of the limited partnership will allow you to determine whether the partnership's goals meet yours. You can gain insight into likely activities of the business and determine whether the partnership fulfills your needs.

Since many limited partnerships are illiquid investments, the general partners intended investment holding period is an important consideration in the decision-making process. Often, the timing of the decision to end the partnership may not be in the best interest of the limited partners.Determining goal compatibility is an effective screening device. Investors must also determine the income-oriented limited partnership's objectives in regard to distributions of cash flow. Will the partnership pay out all available cash, or reinvest the excess cash in additional properties?

Project Description

Limited partnerships can be formed to acquire specific properties or to fund a "blind pool" for future investment opportunities. In the former instance, a prospectus or offering memorandum will describe the investment itself (including its location) and the benefits to be derived from the acquisition, and will provide market comparables in terms of revenues and expenses. In the case of a blind pool, these documents will detail the proposed activities of the partnership.

Sources of Invested Capital

The capital requirements of an investment are provided through the infusion of equity and/or debt. In a limited partnership form, equity contributions may be made by both general and limited partners. However, the limited partners will usually put up the lion's share of the equity, while the general partners contribution is minimal.

The limited partners' equity contributions may be required to be paid in all at once or over an extended period of time depending on the structure of the investment. The length of the limited partners' pay-in period will be influenced by the project's cash operating requirements and by the terms of the project's acquisition. Often, the equity contributions will be used to fund anticipated cash deficits in the early years of an investment. Furthermore, if the partnership's purchase of a property is on an installment basis, the equity contributions can be scheduled to match the purchase obligation.

If the investment has a multiple year pay-in requirement, investors may be required to sign a promissory note for the unpaid portion. The promissory note itself will not increase their basis in the property. However, as investors pay the note off, their contributions increase their basis in the partnership.

In addition to the use of equity, some income-oriented limited partnerships may involve the use of debt. In reviewing the terms of the debt arrangement, investors should address the following questions:

Is the debt of a recourse nature? With recourse financing, the limited partner is personally liable for a portion of the partnership's debt.

Are the terms of the loan favorable? The interest rate on debt should be compared with market rates. If the rate is fixed for the duration of the loan, how does it compare with current rates available? If the rate is of a variable nature, how is it determined? If the rate is tied to an index, you should determine which index it is tied to and what the spread is.

Is the length of the loan considerably longer than the economic life of the investment? Some deals are amortized over periods in excess of the properties' lives simply because the investment cannot support a shorter amortization schedule. Studying the term of loan can also help in evaluating the investment.

Does the debt obligation require a balloon payment? If so, the investment might have to be refinanced at far less favorable rates. Even worse, you may not be able to refinance the property at all. Thus the possibility of default on a loan coupled with a rapid property write-off may leave investors with a substantial tax bill and no cash.

Is the investment too highly leveraged? The level of debt will directly influence the overall riskiness of the investment. One measure of leverage, the *debt-to-asset ratio*, is an indicator of the amount of leverage employed relative to the cost of the property acquired. As discussed in chapter 2, the use of debt increases not only the potential return but also the investment's risk.

Partnership Allocations

Although a particular investment opportunity may be quite attractive, the allocation of partnership items may determine its success from the limited partner's vantage point. The sharing arrangement for cash distributions from operations, refinancing, or disposal of property can offer insight into the fairness of an income-oriented limited partnership. Certain determinations must be made in this area.

Investors must determine whether there is a preferential return of invested capital. This is an important provision in all sharing arrangements. Under such an arrangement, the limited partners would be entitled to a return of their contributed capital before the general partners would be entitled to any cash distributions resulting from operations, refinancing, or disposition of the partnership's properties.

Investors should also determine if the sharing arrangement provides that limited partners be paid interest on their capital contributions as a "preferential return." In addition to it being cumulative, is the interest compounded annually? If it is not compounded, the return will not likely compensate investors for the use of their money.

Investors should examine whether the sharing arrangement changes after the limited partners' receive a certain return or amount of cash. This feature may limit the investment's profit potential.

Finally, any cash distributions to which investors are entitled will only be paid after the partnership meets its normal operating and financial obligations. The extent to which management fees contribute to the required expenses will determine the fairness of the investment. If management fees are excessive, the allocation of cash distributions between the partners is academic.

Compensation to General Partners

The general partners are responsible for carrying on the daily activities of the partnership's business. In addition, they assume an unlimited liability, which is essential for the partnership's treatment of income taxes. Therefore, the general partners deserve to be compensated for engaging in these activities and assuming these risks.

Investors must study the general partners' compensation arrangement carefully. Compensation should be based on the success of the venture to ensure that both the general and limited partners have the same objectives. Investors must determine if the cards are stacked against them before they enter into the investment. Fees based on a percentage of the investment value offer the general partners little incentive and can be a drain on the investment. Heavy back-end fees will limit the cash distribution to the limited partners and thus lower the investment value.

Management History and Prior Records

Do the general partners have a proven record in regard to the management of the contemplated investment? Explore their work history and educational background. Results of past deals will not guarantee future success but can nevertheless be useful.

Pro Forma Estimates

Included in the offering memorandum or prospectus are *pro forma* estimates of the partnership's taxable income, anticipated cash distributions from operations, and cash distributions arising from sale of properties. These projections are made for periods of 15 years or longer. While few people would expect these projections to be based on the condition of certainty, they should still be evaluated based on their underlying assumptions.

In that regard, each item from the forecast income statement should be examined to determine whether its values and trends are realistic. For example, the growth rates for each item of revenue and expense should be compared with the recent past and external forecasts by industry sources. (We will examine the relevant variables as well as where to find comparable information when we examine each type of income-oriented limited partnership.)

Investments that fail to generate positive cash flows during the first few years might still appear attractive due to the forecast of proceeds to be received at the end of the project's life. However, the assumptions concerning the property's appreciation or value over time may be unrealistic. Investors should also examine the underlying assumptions regarding the sale of the property as presented in the financial statements.

A careful evaluation of the likely supply and demand forces will provide insight into the correctness of these projections. Projections of high residual values for computer equipment, for example, may in fact ignore the reality of rapid technological change.

If investors are satisfied with the *pro forma* estimates provided by the sponsor, they should then determine what rate of return to expect, by calculating either the net present value of the investment or its internal rate of return, using the techniques developed in chapter 4. If investors believe the *pro forma* estimates to be overly optimistic, they can substitute their own figures for the ones found in the document's exhibit section. For example, if investors believe that the estimated proceeds from the sale of property is unrealistically high, they can recalculate the return using their own figures.

COMMON OFFERING MEMORANDUM ELEMENTS

The parts of an offering memorandum or prospectus discussed in the following sections are usually boilerplate (the 75 percent mentioned earlier) or generic in nature. Their contents can usually be found in most income-oriented limited partnership investments of similar type. These sections need not be part of the initial screening process, but can be read after the elimination process is completed.

Project Risks

The purpose of this section is to alert the potential investor to all possible risks associated with the project itself or the partnership in general. The section gives the investor a summary of all possible risks associated with investing in the limited partnership units.

This section will identify risks that are associated with the investment being considered. Usually risks involving property ownership, reliance on management, competition, government regulation, lack of diversification, lack of liquidity, and potential conflicts of interest are often cited. (We will detail the sources of risk for each of the more common income-oriented limited partnerships in the chapters that follow.)

Chapter 6

Tax Aspects

This section of an offering memorandum or prospectus will spell out the various tax risks inherent in the investment itself and is designed to alert investors to possible adverse consequences of purchasing units of the offering. Included in this section is the warning that purchase of partnership units may trigger an audit of investors' tax returns, that the partnership may be taxed as a corporation, and that current law might change, thus adversely affecting the value of the investment. (This last point can be appreciated by those investors who purchased shelter-oriented limited partnerships only to have the tax benefits from their expected losses disappear as a result of the passive loss provisions of the Tax Reform Act of 1986.)

A tax risk would arise, for example, if the IRS successfully challenges valuation of the property, thus exposing the investor to possible penalties for overvaluation and understatement of tax liabilities.

Investors also run the risk that the fees paid to the general partners are not deductible but are merely the general partners' share of cash distributions. If the Internal Revenue Service is successful, these fees will be viewed for tax purposes as cash distributions to the general partners. In this instance deductions by the partnership for these fees will be disallowed.

The possible impact of tax preference items will also be addressed—like the fact that investors might be subject to additional tax as a result of being exposed to the alternative minimum tax. Other tax risks (such as the investors' limit regarding investment interest expense deductions, discussed in chapter 2) will also be disclosed in this section of the memorandum.

A summary of the tax aspects cited above is included in this section of the memorandum and provides a legal opinion of these risks. This section discusses the partnership's treatment of certain items of taxation and the legal basis of such treatment. Although it is often vague and full of disclaimers, the tone of the legal opinion can provide clues about possible areas of difficulty.

Limited Partnership Agreement

The limited partnership agreement generally contains a definition of terms; the name, purpose, and term of the partnership; and its place of business. It also defines both the limited and general partners and their liabilities. Another portion of the agreement details allocations between partners of the profits or losses resulting from either sale or refinancing of partnership properties. The agreement also specifies how cash distributions should be allocated. (Appendix E contains the Uniform Limited Partnership Act.)

The partnership agreement also defines the rights, powers, and duties of the partners. This area primarily concerns itself with the management of the business, the authority and/or restrictions of the general partners, and their responsibilities and obligations. The nature and amount of compensation to the general partners is also be included in this section.

The partnership agreement also contains provisions on the transferability of interests, voting rights, and other general partnership provisions.

Suitability Standards

As mentioned earlier, some offerings are exempt from SEC registration as long as they meet certain requirements. Under regulation D, sponsors may offer the units to an unlimited number of "accredited" investors. However, in order to comply with regulation D, sponsors are restricted to a maximum of 35 other "suitable" investors. The suitability standards specify requirements necessary for these investors who are not "accredited" but are deemed suitable for the units offered for sale.

State limits vary regarding both suitability standards and the number of units that can be distributed to nonaccredited but otherwise suitable investors. These suitability standards are usually based on income, net worth, and marginal tax rate requirements.

Subscription Documents

The subscription documents section contains the subscription agreement detailing the payment of the capital contributions, the timing of payments, along with a questionairre to ensure that the investor meets the suitability requirements. This section may also include a promissory note and a security agreement.

SUMMARY

The federal and state governments comprise a two-tier system of securities regulation. The federal concern lies solely with the timely disclosure of relevant information regarding the investment, while the state concern lies also with the fairness of the investment. This additional merit imposes added burdens on the part of the sponsors.

The SEC requires the registration of limited partnership securities, including the filing of a prospectus whenever a public offering takes place. In certain instances, the sponsor can avoid the registration process through meeting the exemption requirements if the offering is either private or limited.

Obtaining federal exemption does not imply that the offering is exempt from state registration. State securities statutes require the sponsors of an offering to meet its requirements in addition to those of the SEC.

Becoming familiar with the contents of a prospectus or private placement memorandum can save you a lot of time in reviewing potential investment opportunities. These documents are usually divided into the following areas: suitability standards, estimated use of proceeds, investment objectives and policies, project description, project risks, tax aspects, sources of invested capital, partnership allocations, compensation to general partners, management history and prior records, *pro forma* estimates, agreement of limited partnership, and the subscription documents. Knowing what to look for in each of these sections will allow the investor to focus on the most important aspects of the transaction.

Chapter 7

Real Estate Limited Partnerships

Real estate limited partnerships are the most popular income-oriented investments available today. Their popularity can be easily understood, as investors in real estate can enjoy attractive tax deductions, tax-free cash distributions, and the potential of a sizable appreciation of property value when it is sold. This chapter provides a brief overview of the growth of real estate limited partnerships and the types of properties in which they invest. It also details several factors necessary for a proper evaluation of a real estate limited partnership.

More money is invested in real estate limited partnerships than in all other limited partnerships combined. Real estate limited partnerships accounted for more than two thirds of the total capital raised by partnerships in 1985. Table 7.1 presents a breakdown of the total partnership market according to investment category. The vast majority of capital was raised through public offerings, which accounted for over 60 percent of the total capital raised by real estate limited partnerships during 1985.

Chapter 7

Real estate limited partnerships invest in a large variety of properties and can be formed to develop new property or to acquire existing property. Real estate limited partnerships usually invest in either commercial or residential property. Commercial real estate holdings might include office buildings, shopping centers, fast food outlets, warehouses, ministorage units, and other similar facilities. Investment in residential properties can range from individual homes to multiunit dwellings, such as apartment buildings.

Real estate limited partnerships can provide the investor with the opportunity of sharing in the appreciation of property. Merely purchasing a real estate limited partnership interest will not guarantee success, however. Each real estate investment is unique and therefore must be carefully scrutinized to determine its potential for profitability. Thus, while real estate can be a very appealing investment, investors must evaluate real estate limited partnerships on a case-by-case basis.

Table 7.1
Total Partnership Market
($ in millions)

	1985	Percent of total
Real Estate	$12,662	66.78
Oil and Gas	2,286	12.06
Equipment Leasing	757	4.99
R&D/Venture Capital	1,009	5.32
Miscellaneous	2,245	11.95
TOTALS	$18,959	100.00%

Source: Limited Partnership Sales Summary 1985, *The Stanger Review,* p.1.

VALUE ANALYSIS

The evaluation of a real estate limited partnership begins with a determination of the market value of the property. Investors' potential after-tax return is influenced by the price that they pay for the property. If the property is overvalued, then appreciation would be less likely than if the property were either underpriced or priced correctly. Overvaluation results in a lower after-tax return to investors.

Comparable data is available for each type of real estate investment. Investors should compare the prices in the prospectus with the comparable prices to determine if the property has been marked up.

Location

The most important determinant of real estate value is its location. Table 7.2 presents industrial land prices in selected United States cities as of December 1985. As seen from the table, land prices vary considerably, with the lowest prices in the midwest region and the highest prices in the coastal areas.

Property values also vary within each locale. Property situated in a declining suburban location, for example, cannot be expected to appreciate as rapidly as property in a more rapidly developing downtown area. Because of this, screening real estate limited partnerships according to their relative location within each locale is extremely important.

One of the key factors affecting real estate value in general is the location's demographic characteristics. Investors must first determine if the subject property is within a region experiencing an attractive population growth rate, with high employment and attractive per capita income statistics. Table 7.3 shows the employment (nonagricultural) growth from 1984 to 1985 in selected states.

Table 7.2
Industrial Land Prices
Selected United States Cities

	Price per square foot
Boston	$2.00 - $ 3.00
Philadelphia	1.75 - 3.00
Baltimore	1.90 - 2.10
Atlanta	1.40 - 2.00
Tampa	2.50 - 3.50
Miami	4.00 - 6.00
Cincinnati	1.00 - 1.10
Chicago	3.00 - 4.00
Minneapolis	1.00 - 3.00
St. Louis	1.75 - 2.25
Houston	2.25 - 3.50
Dallas	3.50 - 4.50
Kansas City	1.50 - 2.25
Denver	2.50 - 3.50
Seattle-Bellevue	4.25 - 6.00
Portland	2.00 - 3.00
Oakland	4.50 - 5.50
San Jose	6.00 - 8.00
Los Angeles-Orange Counties	7.00 - 9.00
Phoenix	3.00 - 5.00
San Diego	6.00 - 10.00

Note: Typical price paid per square foot for three to five acreswarehouse/distribution land, rail served, fully improved, located in the top district area of the city.

Source: Coldwell Banker Real Estate Consultation Services.

Investors should also assess the economic stability of the investment property's region. For example, they should determine whether the locale is dependent on an individual industry for its continued prosperity. If this is the case, the property value could be adversely influenced should the industry decide

Table 7.3
Employment Growth (1984-1985)

Rankings	Thousands of jobs
1. California	251
2. Florida	220
3. New York	146
4. Texas	139
5. Georgia	127
6. Massachusetts	125
7. Ohio	105
8. New Jersey	101
9. Michigan	100
10. Maryland	78
11. Arizona	73
12. Virginia	69
13. Pennsylvania	62
14. Indiana	52
15. Minnesota	51
16. South Carolina	50
17. North Carolina	44
18. Wisconsin	39
19. Illinois	36
20. Tennessee	33
21. Connecticut	29
22. Kentucky	29
23. New Hampshire	28
24. Colorado	23
25. Kansas	20

Source: U.S. Bureau of Labor Statistics, Employment and Earnings 1986.

to relocate or if it experiences economic problems. This risk has been evidenced during the recent times, where the effects of the oil industry collapse has been felt in the real estate market. Housing prices plummeted, as banks foreclosed on homeowners victimized by oil industry layoffs. The commercial market was also adversely affected.

Investors should evaluate the likely role of government and its effect on real estate values. They must determine the impact of present and future tax policies as they relate to the property's value. This aspect not only includes an assessment of the possibilities of property taxes increases, but increases in other state and/or local transfer taxes as well. Furthermore, local government's attitude toward rent control or other income-limiting restrictions will also have an influence on the potential of a given property.

Efficiency Ratio

Many of the smaller private placements of real estate limited partnerships involve the purchase of a single building. In these instances, the investor can evaluate the building itself. A building's value will be influenced by its overall design and engineering attributes. One common measure used in judging the design features of a building is called the efficiency ratio. The *efficiency ratio* compares a building's net leasable square feet with its gross square feet. The higher the ratio, the more efficient the building is said to be. For example, if a building were to have an efficiency ratio of 75 percent, it would indicate that 25 percent of the gross building area is unleasable.

Buildings which have efficiency ratios of less than 85 percent are not economical due to the large amount of unleasable space and therefore should be avoided. Since in many urban areas land cost is prohibitive, the building's efficiency level can be major determinant of the investment's likely success. Low efficiency ratios can make otherwise marginal investments fail.

Loan-to-Value Ratio

In most leveraged real estate investments, the lending institution will provide funds based on the project's expected cash flow up to a certain percent of the property's value. A loan-to-value ratio is used to determine the extent of a lender's participation. The loan-to-value ratio is found by dividing the dollar amount of debt by the value of the property. Typically a lender will provide funds up to 80 percent of the estimated value of the property.

PROPERTY APPRAISALS

Often, the lending institution will obtain the services of a real estate appraiser to determine the value of the property under consideration. The appraiser determines the property's value using any of following three approaches: market comparison, income, and cost.

Market-Comparison Approach

Many real estate professionals rely on the market-comparison approach in determining if the property under consideration is correctly priced. The market-comparison approach involves the comparison of the subject property with similar properties that have sold recently in comparable locations. The appraiser determines the subject property's value through such comparables as age, size, quality of construction, layout and location.

Income Approach

Another technique used by appraisers to determine real estate value is the income approach. Under the income approach, the appraiser may determine value through the use of an overall capitalization rate or a gross rent multiplier. If the former technique is used, the appraiser divides the property's operating income by a capitalization rate which would reflect an

Chapter 7

investor's required return. (Table 7.4 illustrates how the capitalization rate technique works.)

Market Value Estimation
Capitalization Rate Approach

Property	#1	#2
Net operating income	$ 100,000	$ 120,000
Capitalization rate	.10	.10
Market value	$1,000,000	$1,200,000

If a property had a net operating income totaling $100,000 and the capitalization rate was ten percent, the property would be appraised at $1,000,000 ($100,000/.10). If the property's net operating income wereforecast to be $120,000, its value would be $1,200,000. The overall riskiness of the investment would influence the capitalization rate chosen. High-risk projects would be capitalized at a high rate, while low-risk projects would be capitalized at a low rate.

Table 7.5 shows the average capitalization rates for major office, retail, and industrial properties during the period from 1982 through 1985 as compiled by Coldwell Banker Commercial Real Estate Services. During that time, the overall capitalization for office buildings and shopping centers have declined; the capitalization rate for industrial space, on the other hand, increased.

Another valuation method similar to the capitalization rate approach is the use of a gross rent multiplier. This method of determines the value of real estate relative to other properties based on a multiple of the property's gross rents. The multiplier can be used to determine whether a given property is properly priced. Table 7.6 illustrates this technique.

Suppose that a property generated $200,000 in gross rents

Table 7.5
Capitalization Rates for
Office, Retail, and Industrial Property
(1982-1985)

Office Buildings

Year	Percentage
1982	9.4%
1983	8.4
1984	8.3
1985E	7.9

Industrial Space

1982	8.4%
1983	8.6
1984	9.8
1985E	9.6

Shopping Centers

1982	8.3%
1983	8.2
1984	8.1
1985E	7.6

Note: Average capitalization rates of sales handled by Coldwell Banker. Averages are not weighted. Major properties include all properties sold for $10 million or more, except industrial.

Source: Coldwell Banker Commercial Real Estate Services.

Table 7.6
Market Value Estimation
Gross Rent Multiplier

	Low Range	
Property	A	B
Gross rents earned	$ 200,000	$ 400,000
Gross rents multiplier	6	6
Market value	$1,200,000	$2,400,000
	High Range	
Property	A	B
Gross rents earned	$ 200,000	$ 400,000
Gross rents multiplier	8	8
Market value	$1,600,000	$3,200,000

annually and that comparable properties have recently sold at gross rent multipliers of between six and eight. As shown in table 7.6, this would suggest that the price range is between $1,200,000 and $1,600,000. This tool enables investors to compare projects on relative terms.

It is important to remember that the gross rent multiplier is just a rough indicator of real estate value. For example, a high gross rent multiplier may be justified based on the property's appreciation potential and/or on its attractive tax benefits (historic restorations).

Cost Approach

A final method utilized by real estate appraisers is the cost approach. Under this approach, the cost of replacing the property is used as an indicator of value. The appraiser estimates the cost per square foot of reconstructing of the facility. For those calculations, the appraiser evaluates the property's physical condition and the degree of functional obsolescence, to arrive at a value.

This can be a particularly valuable tool for investors in determining if the property is priced properly. For example, if the limited partnership is planning on constructing an office building, the cost of construction (per square foot) should be compared with that of other similar projects. If construction costs are high by comparison, this probably indicates that the project is not viable as an investment. Data is readily available for commercial property as well as for residential property.

Based on one or a combination of all of these real estate valuation approaches, the appraiser estimates the value of a piece of property. The appraised value then becomes the measure of value lenders will use to determine the extent of their investment. Investors should expect the prospectus or private

offering memorandum to contain a detailed appraisal on each
property contained in the package.

REVENUE ANALYSIS

To determine whether an investment is attractive on a com-
parative basis, investors must next determine if the project's
revenue stream forecast is reasonable. A detailed market
analysis can tell investors whether the property's projected
revenues are realistic when compared to those of other properties in the marketplace. For example, if a limited partnership
forecasts an office building's monthly rental income based on
$35 per square foot, when comparable office space leases for
$25 per square foot, the project is probably not viable.

In the case of residential property, if rents are forecasted to
be $350 per unit in an area where apartments of comparable
value range from $250 to $300, the investment may not be
worthwhile. It is extremely important that investors be familiar with the market where the property is situated.

The private offering memorandum will usually contain a
market survey detailing comparable rents. Investors must
make sure that the rates contained in the sponsor's financial
statements are in line with market rates.

The rental value of real estate is influenced greatly by the
balance between supply and demand. If, for example, supply is
high while demand is soft (low), the property may be vacant
for some time. An area's vacancy rate can provide valuable
information about the market's rental demand. Vacancy rates
are provided by an number of organizations and are available
to investors. Table 7.7 presents the vacancy rates for downtown, metropolitan, and suburban areas for selected cities.

A large number of vacancies can be particularly bothersome
for real estate limited partnerships involved in the construction of speculative property (less than 20 percent leased),

Chapter 7

which must be evaluated on its forecast leaseup. The presence of a large number of speculative buildings can have an adverse effect on rental rates; other existing properties may be adversely affected and therefore unable to increase rents.

Table 7.7
Office Vacancy Rates for Selected Cities
(December 1985)

City	Downtown	Metropolitan	Suburban
Atlanta	12.8%	18.6%	20.0%
Boston	10.7	14.1	18.8
Chicago	10.6	14.5	21.7
Cincinnati	17.4	19.0	22.1
Dallas	17.5	24.3	26.9
Denver	26.0	26.1	26.2
Houston	20.2	28.2	31.0
Los Angeles	18.2	16.9	16.6
Miami	19.5	20.3	20.6
Minneapolis/St. Paul	13.9	17.7	22.3
Philadelphia	10.2	14.5	19.3
Phoenix	18.8	25.4	29.2
St Louis	10.8	10.3	9.9
Tampa	25.9	26.3	26.4
Washington, D.C.	9.7	11.1	14.0

Source: Coldwell Banker Commercial Real Estate Services.

The demand for rental property can be ascertained by studying the market itself. Professional leasing firms gauge a property's leasing prospects by determining what they call the market's "absorption rate." The absorption rate is an estimate of the total number of square feet of new property that can be accommodated during a given period of time. For instance, a market may have an absorption rate of 200,000 square feet of office space per year. This means that the market can support this yearly increase in the supply of office buildings. By comparing this figure with the schedule of new office developments, investors can determine the potential risk of either vacancies or sluggish rental growth.

Knowledge of the absorption rate can be very beneficial for evaluating projects which are speculative in nature. For example, if a new office building is being planned, absorption rate data can provide information such as the time necessary to lease the facility. A low absorption rate coupled with a market glut can result in the property being vacant over an extended period of time.

OPERATING COSTS ANALYSIS

In addition to evaluating the likely rental income from a real estate project, investors need to determine if projected costs are reasonable when compared to similar existing properties. For example, the project's forecasted operating expenses should be compared to those of similar facilities in the same market. If these costs rise at a faster rate than was assumed by the syndicator, the project may experience lower margins and may not be able to produce the desired cash flow. Thus, not only should the initial cost estimates be accurate, but the growth assumptions must be on target as well.

The terms of the lease agreement, for example, will specify who is responsible for the various expenses required to operate the facility.Sometimes the increase in operating expenses can be shared by the tenant. In this situation, the partnership might be required to pay a base amount of operating expenses, with any additional amount to be paid by the tenant or leasee.

If the parties enter into a triple net lease arrangement, the maintenance, insurance, and property tax payments are borne by the leasee. If on the other hand the leasor (limited partnership) is responsible for meeting these expenses, the risk is borne by the leasor. An unforeseen increase in insurance costs, for example, may reduce profits significantly.

Chapter 7

Financing Expenses

Real estate limited partnerships may be unleveraged or leveraged. In the unleveraged limited partnerships, investor capital will fund the entire project, while leveraged limited partnerships may employ a sizable amount of debt. The debt arrangement in a leveraged investment plays a significant role in the overall success of most real estate limited partnerships. In these latter types of partnerships, it is not uncommon for total debt to account for 80 percent or more of the property's value. Purchase money financing (seller financing) will often supplement first mortgage arrangements, increasing the leverage even further.

Investors must examine the attractiveness of the terms of the debt financing arrangement. For example, the loan's interest rate requirements should be compared with present rates available in the marketplace. If the partnership is able to assume a mortgage which is considerably below market, the value of the investment will be enhanced.

The interest payments may be based on either a fixed or variable rate basis. An increasing number of lenders are requiring borrowers to assume the risk of rising interest rates through the use of variable rate financing. Typically, variable rate loans require that the interest rate be tied to an index, such as a major bank's prime lending rate, with the partnership required to pay a specified percentage above that rate.

Changes in interest rates could be accommodated either by adjusting periodic payments or by adjusting the principal balance. If the latter arrangement is entered into, a sizable amount of the property's appreciation will be used to retire the mortgage balance, leaving little to distribute to limited partners desiring cash to settle their capital gain recognition.

Investors must determine the loan's amortization period and evaluate the partnership's ability to service the debt requirements. The longer the amortization period, the lower the monthly debt service requirements. Many projects are not viable unless the amortization period is unusually long. This may indicate that the project cannot generate sufficient cash flow to service debt without this increase in amortization period and therefore may not be worthwhile.

One way to determine the risk of default is to compare the partnership's forecast revenues with those necessary to cover all cash requirements, or to break even. How close are the forecast amounts to those required to break even?

TAX CONSIDERATIONS

Once investors have determined that the acquisition price is reasonable, they must investigate the tax benefits associated with the investment. These advantages may enable investors to increase their after-tax return, by allowing them to receive partially tax-free cash disbursements.

Depreciation

The first tax advantage offered by real estate is the use of depreciation, a periodic write-off of the costs of improved property (buildings). This expense can be taken over a 27.5-year period in the case of residential properties and 31.5 years for nonresidential properties. It can therefore generate tax benefits for the limited partners. Investors are allowed to take these write-offs against the project's revenues even though the property will most likely increase in value over time.

Under the Tax Reform Act of 1986, the partnership must depreciate the property under the straight-line method, and the yearly depreciation schedule is determined by the month the asset is placed in service.

Chapter 7

Rehabilitation Tax Credits

The Tax Reform Act of 1986 enables taxpayers to apply Rehabilitation Tax Credits (RTC) against the cost of substantial renovation of qualified income-producing property. The rehabilitation tax credit is a dollar-for-dollar reduction of the tax liability. Hence, its value to taxpayers is independent of their marginal tax rate. The dollar amount of the RTC received can be found by multiplying the asset's renovation expenditures by the applicable rate.

The applicable RTC rate depends on the type of project under consideration. For projects that qualify as historic renovations, the amount of RTC is equal to 20 percent of the cost of rehabilitation without regard to age. In addition to the historic rehabilitation credit, the Tax Reform Act of 1986 permits an RTC if the property was originally placed into service prior to 1936. In both cases, the asset's depreciable base must be reduced by the dollar amount of the RTC.

To qualify for the rehabilitation tax credit, 75 percent of the building's walls must be retained (as either interior or exterior walls), at least 50 percent of the exterior walls must continue to be used as exterior walls, and at least 75 percent of the interior structure must be retained.

Alternative Minimum Tax

The impact of the real estate limited partnership's use of tax preference items subject to the alternative minimum tax must also considered by investors. The extent to which a partnership generates deductions that are items of tax preference may limit its desired results. Investors, in making sure that their overall tax liability is reduced, must be aware of their tax liability as computed using the alternative minimum tax method.

Investment Interest Expense Limitation

In chapter 2, we stated that the deductibility of investment interest is limited. Investors must determine the dollar amount of investment interest expense per each limited partnership unit. The amount of investment interest expense will sometimes be disclosed in the prospectus. If not, investors should determine its affect before entering into the partnership.

ORGANIZATIONAL EXPENSES

The partnership will have certain costs associated with forming and organizing the partnership. Investor must determine the reasonableness of these costs in relation to the size and scope of the project. If the fees in these larger limited partnerships represent more than seven percent of the equity capital investment, the project may not be worthwhile.

SECURITIES COMMISSIONS

Real estate limited partnership units are usually sold by registered representatives employed by brokerage firms. The partnership will pay sales commissions to these individuals for their efforts. The sales commissions, paid out of investor proceeds, can range from three to ten percent (sometimes higher). Sales commissions in excess of eight percent of the funds being raised should be discouraged.

GENERAL PARTNERS' FEES

General partners may also be compensated for managing the property, leasing space, and general administration. While these expenses may contribute to investors' exposure to taxes, they ultimately have the effect of reducing the value of the investment.

A properly structured partnership is one where the general partners are compensated based on performance of their duties. It is best to avoid limited partnerships in which the general partners are heavily compensated at the beginning of the transaction. Such front-loading of fees will provide the general partners with little incentive to achieve the longer term goals of the limited partners. Management fees of more than five percent of the gross revenues are excessive.

Investors should also make sure that the fees at the time of asset disposal are not excessive. Fees earned by the general partners as part of the property's disposal, such as real estate commissions, will reduce the limited partners' return. Limited partners should therefore be aware of the general partners' compensation arrangement at the time of sale.

SHARING ARRANGEMENT

The sharing arrangement between the limited and general partners can influence whether a good property investment translates into a good investment for the limited partners. It has sometimes been said that the role of a limited partnership sponsor is to transform an attractive investment into a marginal limited partnership. As mentioned in chapter 6, the partnership agreement will detail the sharing arrangement between the general partners and limited partners in regard to cash flow, book profits, and net appreciation.

Profits and losses

Typically, real estate limited partnerships will designate as much as 90 percent of the partnership losses (and profits) to the limited partners in return for their investment. (Remember that losses from any partnerships entered into after the enactment of the Tax Reform Act of 1986 can only be used to offset other passive income.)

Cash Flow from Operations

The general partners in all likelihood will not be as generous when it comes to cash flow. Limited partners should be given a preferential return based on their capital contribution prior to any significant distributions to the general partners. However, it is not uncommon for the general partners in a limited partnership to be allocated as much as 20 percent of the partnerships' cash distribution from operations. Partnerships in which the general partners (with little or no investment) receive more than 20 percent of these cash distributions should be avoided.

Reversion

The sharing arrangement in regard to the disposal of the investment property is also important in the evaluation of a limited partnership. Investors should make sure that they are entitled to a preferential return of their original capital investment, plus interest on their investment.

Investors should limit their search to limited partnerships that provide a preferential return of their capital, including interest payments at market rates. In some instances, the partnership agreement might specify that the limited partners must receive a minimum cash on cash return before the general partners are entitled to any profits.

Chapter 7

LIMITED PARTNERS' PAY-IN

A real estate limited partnership may require either a single pay-in or a pay-in over several years. Most public real estate limited partnerships require a single payment of equity. Smaller private offerings may require investors to contribute capital for a period of four years or longer.

SUMMARY

Real estate investments have enjoyed unparalleled success as income-oriented limited partnerships. The attractive depreciation tax benefits enabling investors to receive tax-free cash flows have made real estate one of the most popular income-oriented investments available today.

Investors must determine whether the acquisition price of a limited partnership's property is fair and reasonable. Many limited partnerships provide an independent appraisal of the property for investor inspection. The appraiser uses a market, income, or cost approach in determining the fair market value of the property.

Each real estate investment is unique and therefore must be examined on an individual basis. Investors must fully understand the underlying assumptions concerning revenue and operating costs estimates. In addition, investors should screen out investments where the sharing arrangement favors the general partners or where indirect acquisition costs appear to be excessive.

Chapter 8

Analysis Of An Apartment Complex Real Estate Syndication

A real estate limited partnership's investment value is based on its cash flow pattern during its operations phase, its sheltering capabilities, and its reversion value. Each of these components contributes to the investment's overall after-tax rate of return. The task of investors is to determine whether the price asked by the syndicator for these components is fair.

Investors can accomplish this task by evaluating the real estate limited partnership in terms of the likely realization of the investment's after-tax cash flows and net appreciation assumptions. The starting point is the analysis of the limited partnership's *pro forma* (forecast) financial statements.

APARTMENT BUILDING SYNDICATION ILLUSTRATION

In order to demonstrate the concept of a real estate syndication, we will consider an investment in a hypothetical apartment building limited partnership. Table 8.1 presents the assumptions underlying the real estate partnership.

Table 8.1
Apartment Complex Limited Partnership Assumptions

Number of units offered	200
Total equity raised	$6,650,000
Equity contribution per limited partnership unit	33,250
Cost of apartment units	6,000,000
Securities commissions (8 percent)	532,000
Organizational expenses (amortized over 60 months)	118,000
Assumed Value (year 7)	8,750,000
Selling expenses	3%
Operating expenses (as a percent of revenue)	15%
Limited partner's tax bracket	28%
Limited partners' share of profits (losses)	99%
General partners' share of profits (losses)	1%
Limited partners' share of cash distributions	99%
General partners' share of cash distributions	1%
Limited partners' share of residual cash flow	99%
General partners' share of residual cash flow	1%

PROFIT AND LOSS STATEMENTS

Table 8.2 presents the partnerships' forecast profit (loss) statements from years one through six based on the information contained in table 8.1 and other assumptions. Those other assumptions underlying the forecast profit and loss statements are given below.

Revenue is forecast to be $575,000 in year one and is expected to increase at a rate of six percent per annum. Organizational expenses of $118,000 are amortized over the first five years at an annual rate of $23,600. Operating expenses represent 15 percent (including leasing expenses) of rental income.

The partnership's profit represents rental income less the sum of organizational, operating, and depreciation expenses. The partnership's tax liability can be found by multiplying the yearly profits by 28 percent. The limited partners tax liability is equal to 99 percent of the total tax liability and can be found on the last line of table 8.2.

Table 8.2
Apartment Complex Profit (Loss) Statements
(28 percent tax bracket)

Year	1	2	3
Rental income	$575,000	$609,500	$646,070
Less:			
Organizational expenses	23,600	23,600	23,600
Operating expenses	86,250	91,425	96,911
Depreciation expenses	196,364	196,364	196,364
Total expenses	$306,214	$311,389	$316,875
Profit	$268,786	$298,111	$329,195
Total tax liability	$ 75,260	$ 83,471	$ 92,175
Limited partners' share (99%)	$ 74,507	$ 82,636	$ 91,253

Year	4	5	6
Rental income	$684,834	$725,924	$769,479
Less:			
Organizational expenses	23,600	23,600	
Operating expenses	102,725	108,887	115,422
Depreciation expenses	196,364	196,364	196,364
Total expenses	$322,689	$328,851	$311,786
Profit	$362,145	$397,073	$457,693
Total tax liability	$101,401	$111,180	$128,154
Limited partners' share (99%)	$100,387	$110,068	$126,872

Table 8.3 presents the yearly tax liability per each limited partnership unit. The investor's initial contribution of $33,250 is found by dividing the total investors' contributions ($6,650,000) by the number of units offered (200). The yearly tax liability per individual unit is found by dividing the last line of table 8.2 by the number of units offered.

Table 8.3
Yearly Tax Liability
(28 percent tax bracket)

Year	Initial outlay	Tax liability
0	($33,250)	-
1		$ 373
2		413
3		456
4		502
5		550
6		634
	($33,250)	$ 2,928

CASH DISTRIBUTIONS

Rental income less total cash disbursements (operating expenses) represent the partnership's distributive cash. The limited partners, according to the sharing arrangement, are allocated 99 percent of the partnership's distributive cash. The limited partners' cash flows from operations are found in table 8.4. The last line of table 8.4 represents the limited partners' share of the partnership's cash distribution.

Table 8.5 presents the cash distribution per limited partnership unit. The yearly cash flow per individual unit is found by dividing the last line of table 8.4 by the number of units offered (200). The table reveals that an initial investment by the limited partner of $33,250 results in cash distributions totaling $16,874 during the initial six-year period.

Table 8.4
Cash Flow Statements

Year	1	2	3
Rental income	$575,000	$609,500	$646,070
Less:			
Operating expenses	86,250	91,425	96,911
Distributed cash	$488,750	$518,075	$549,160
Limited P's share (99%)	$483,863	$512,894	$543,668

Year	4	5	6
Rental income	$684,834	$725,924	$769,480
Less:			
Operating expenses	102,725	108,889	115,422
Distributive cash	$582,109	$617,035	$654,058
Limited P's share (99%)	$576,288	$610,865	$647,517

Table 8.5
Yearly Cash Flow

Year	Initial investment	Cash flow
1	($33,250)	$ 2,419
2		2,564
3		2,718
4		2,881
5		3,054
6		3,238
TOTALS	($33,250)	$16,874

CASH DISTRIBUTIONS: SALE OF APARTMENT BUILDING

In addition to the cash distributions during the operating phase of the investment, the limited partners are also entitled to 99 percent of the proceeds from the sale of the apartment complex. Table 8.6 shows the calculations for the before-tax reversion, assuming the apartment complex is sold in year seven for $8,750,000 less selling expenses equaling three percent.

Table 8.6
Before-Tax Reversion

Sale price	$8,750,000
Less:	
Selling expenses	262,500
Net sale price	$8,487,500
Limited partners cash distribution (99%)	8,402,625
Per limited partner	$ 42,013

Each individual limited partner would receive $42,013 ($8,402,625/200) at the time the asset is sold. However, investors must still pay taxes based on this distribution and their own adjusted basis.

PARTNER'S BASIS CALCULATIONS

The individual partner's initial basis in this example is an equity contribution ($33,250). The partner's basis will be altered by one of the following: (1) capital contributions (increase), (2) taxable income of the partnership (increase), (3) borrowing by the partnership (increase), (4) partnership losses (decrease), (5) distributions of partnership property (decrease), or (6) reduction in the amount of partnership debt (decrease).

Table 8.7 demonstrates the calculation of a limited partners' capital account at the end of year 6. Their basis is found by adding their share of the partnerships' profits less any cash distributions from their initial contributions. Based on the calculations shown in table 8.7, you can see that the limited partner's adjusted basis is $26,836.

Table 8.7
Limited Partner's Adjusted Capital Account

(1)	(2)	(3)	(4)	(5)
				(2 + 3 - 4)
	Equity	Profit	Cash	Adjusted
Year	investment	(losses)	distribution	basis
1	$33,250	$ 1,330	$ 2,419	
2		1,476	2,564	
3		1,630	2,718	
4		1,793	2,881	
5		1,966	3,054	
6		2,266	3,238	
TOTALS	$33,250	$10,461	$16,875	$26,836

Table 8.8 presents the after-tax reversion per limited partner. Since the limited partners' capital account is positive, they must subtract their basis from that amount to their cash distribution to arrive at their profit on sale of the apartment complex.

Table 8.8
After-Tax Reversion Per Limited Partner

Cash distribution	$ 42,013
Less:	
Adjusted basis of limited partner	26,836
Gain on sale	$ 15,177
Total liability (28% of gain on sale price)	4,250
After-tax reversion per limited partner	$ 37,763

Limited partners receive $42,013 from the sale of the apartment. Their total profit is calculated to be $15,177 ($42,013 – $26,836). The tax on this profit would be $4,250, leaving an after-tax reversion per limited partner of $37,763 ($42,438 – $4,250).

Table 8.9 summarizes the components of the limited partners' after-tax return. Now that we have identified the limited partner's expected tax liability, cash distribution, and after-tax reversion, we can calculate their after-tax return.

Table 8.9
Limited Partner Return
($33,250 per unit)

Year	Sum invested	Tax liability	Cash flows	Due at reversion	Cumulative amounts
0	($33,250)				($33,250)
1		$ 373	$2,419		2,046
2		413	2,564		2,151
3		456	2,718		2,262
4		502	2,881		2,379
5		550	3,054		2,504
6		634	3,238		2,604
7				37,763	37,763
TOTAL					$18,459

IRR = 7.67%

NPV(8%) = -$544.

The investor's after-tax return or internal rate of return (IRR) is calculated to be 7.67 percent, while the net present value is -$544 (at eight percent). If investors required a return greater than eight percent, they would reject the deal. Investors must weigh the various project risks versus the above return. Then they must determine whether the expected after-tax return from the investment compares favorably with the return and risks of other investment opportunities.

SUMMARY

While real estate as an investment has performed well historically, there are no guarantees that individuals contemplating acquiring limited partnership interests will be successful. Inflated property values cannot be expected to appreciate at the same rate as correctly priced properties. Investors must determine the probable amount of tax liability, cash flow, and after-tax reversion from their participation in a real estate limited partnership. The assumptions underlying the financial statements must be evaluated on their reasonableness and accuracy. Only then can investors calculate their expected after-tax return from an investment.

Chapter 9

Mortgage Limited Partnerships

Mortgage limited partnerships offer investors the opportunity of investing in real estate on an indirect basis. These partnerships pool individual investor funds for the purpose of financing the acquisition of real estate mortgage debt instruments. The terms of mortgages held by these partnerships are dependent upon the objectives of the sponsors. This chapter reviews the most common types of debt-oriented limited partnerships.

TYPES OF MORTGAGE LIMITED PARTNERSHIPS

Mortgage limited partnerships may invest in a variety of mortgages, such as standard, guaranteed, participating, or tax-exempt mortgages. Each of these will have a direct impact the return and risk to be expected by the limited partner.

Standard Mortgages

A standard mortgage would be a taxable obligation where the borrower would secure the loan by pledging the real estate property as collateral. The interest on these mortgages could be either fixed or variable.

Guaranteed Payment Mortgages

Guaranteed payment mortgages consist of mortgages in which the interest and principal are assured by a government agency. At the federal level, these mortgages would normally be backed by a credit facility such as FHA insurance or GNMA Securities, and at the local level, these mortgages would be guaranteed by the taxing authority of the issuing municipality.

Participation Loans

The participation loan has gained popularity over the past few years. Typically, the limited partnership would be provided with loans below the market rate, with amortization periods similar to those available with ordinary fixed-rate financing. These loans might be priced at two percent below prevailing rates, for example. Under these arrangements, the lender would also be entitled to a certain percent of cash flow from operations, profit from refinancing, and/or sale of the assets.

Participating mortgages possess advantages and disadvantages for both the borrower and the limited partnership. From the borrowers' perspective, their loan repayment requirements would be less burdensome. However, their profit potential would be somewhat limited, since the lender will share in the project's success. The limited partnership, in turn, would have the opportunity of sharing in the profits of the venture without taking on the risk of ownership. However, if the project is marginal, the lenders would have committed funds to a project in which their return would be less than that otherwise available in the marketplace.

Tax-Exempt Mortgages

A mortgage limited partnership can be formed to invest in tax-exempt revenue mortgage bonds. These mortgages would be exempt from federal taxation (although investors may be subject to the alternative minimum tax), and in many cases are exempt from state taxation. The payment of principal and interest would be contingent upon the revenues from the project which is being financed by the sale of these mortgages.

ADVANTAGES OF MORTGAGE LIMITED PARTNERSHIPS

There are several advantages associated with investing in mortgage limited partnerships, such as the use of knowledgeable professionals and the benefits of diversification.

Knowledgeable Management

The general partners are responsible for carrying out the daily operations of the limited partnership. These individuals are responsible for screening mortgage investment opportunities. The partnership's ability to utilize the services of knowledgeable professionals will determine its success.

Diversification

Mortgage limited partnerships can provide investors with a high degree of risk reduction through diversification. This is because the investment policy of many trusts requires geographic as well as property-type diversification.

Many mortgage limited partnerships spread their holdings over wide geographic areas. The benefits of geographic diversification have recently been seen in areas such as Texas, where the oil industry decline has adversely affected both the commercial and the residential real estate market. Housing prices plummeted as banks foreclosed on homeowners victimized by oil industry layoffs.

The investment policies of mortgage limited partnerships require that a portfolio of different types of real estate, be maintained and are therefore less susceptible to economic shocks. Partnerships that concentrate their holdings on office buildings in overdeveloped areas may face similar problems in the near future as the supply in many regions has far outpaced the demand. Thus, the diversification aspect of partnerships can be an attractive incentive for the average investor who cannot obtain adequate diversification through direct lending.

INVESTMENT RISKS

While there are advantages associated with investing in mortgage limited partnerships, there are also many risks involved. These risks include the underlying business risk of the investment itself (credit risk), as well as the risk associated with receiving a fixed rate (money rate and purchasing power rate risks) on the funds employed.

Credit Risk

Mortgage limited partnerships invest indirectly by lending funds for construction and/or permanent mortgages. The quality of its debt holdings is a significant factor in the overall success of most mortgage limited partnerships. Certain mortgages—commercial second mortgages, for example—can be expected to provide the partnership with high current yields, but they may also expose the trust to high risk.

In assessing the credit worthiness of a debt-oriented limited partnership, one must examine certain other considerations to judge the overall risk and return of a venture. The borrowing of funds creates two important obligations. First, the borrower must pay the partnership interest on the funds borrowed. Second, the borrower must pay back the loan. It is important to fully understand the essential conditions of the loan as it relates to these two commitments.

Payment of Interest In regard to the first obligation, the terms of the interest rate requirement must be examined. Generally speaking, interest rates may either be fixed or floating. *Fixed-rate financing* means that the rate of interest will not vary over the term of the loan. A *floating loan*, on the other hand, is tied to an index, such as the prime rate or 90-day Treasury-bill rate. Payments are adjusted periodically, usually on either a quarterly or yearly basis.

Under fixed-rate financing, the risk associated with changing interest rates falls largely upon the lender. If rates rise, the partnership will miss the opportunity of lending at a higher rate. If rates fall, borrowers may be able to refinance at these lower rates. Conversely, with floating rates, the partnership's interest charges are adjusted to enable it to realize current yields. Borrowers are at the mercy of market rate fluctuations. Due to these factors, fixed-rate financing alternatives will at first cost more than its variable, or floating rate, counterpart. However, under variable rate financing, borrowers are fully exposed to rising interest rates, so this method of financing may be more costly in the long run.

In addition to periodic interest payments, the partnership will usually require the borrower to pay "points" at time of settlement. A *point* represents one percent of the amount of funds borrowed. This enables the partnership to receive higher yields by requiring the borrower to pay a portion of the interest up front. The number of points charged by the partnership varies depending on the attractiveness of the project and on general market conditions.

Repayment of Principal The second obligation, the repayment of the loan principal, may be accomplished in many ways. Sometimes a partnership will not require repayment until the end of the loan term. Usually the partnership requires periodic repayment of the loan, commonly called *amortization*. This can be accomplished by requiring that the borrower either make equal principal payments or make level payments over the life of the loan. Under the latter arrangement, the total payments are constant, but the principal payments increase over the life of the loan while the interest payments decrease by a like amount so that total payments remain level.

In addition, the partnership may be willing to amortize the loan over a long period but will require total payment within this amortization period. For example, a commercial loan may call for a steady payment with a 30-near amortization. However, it may contain a "balloon" feature which may require the borrower to repay the entire loan at the end of, say, five years, while still figuring the payments until then based on a 30-year amortization schedule. The maximum length of the repayment period will be influenced by the expected life of the asset to be financed, general credit conditions, and the financial strength of the borrower.

The advantage to a balloon loan is that borrowers know what their debt requirements will be, and the partnership has not locked them into a fixed rate for a prolonged period. At the balloon payment date, borrowers can either renegotiate the terms of the loan or refinance it through another source. Borrowers run the risk that rates will be higher at that time or that they will not be able to refinance the loan at all.

Purchasing Power Risk

Purchasing power risk refers to the inability of the mortgage limited partnership's return to keep pace with inflation. The failure of the yield on the partnership's mortgage portfolio to outpace inflation results in reduced purchasing power of the dollars returned to the limited partners. Table 9.1 depicts the inflation rate as measured by the consumer price index.

Table 9.1
Consumer Price Index

Year	CPI
1986	1.10
1985	3.77
1984	3.95
1983	3.80
1982	3.87
1981	8.94
1980	12.40
1979	13.31
1978	9.03
1977	6.77
1976	4.81
1975	7.01
1974	12.20
1973	8.80
1972	3.41
1971	3.36
1970	5.49
1969	6.11
1968	4.72
1967	3.04
1966	3.35
1965	1.92
1964	1.04
1963	1.65
1962	1.22
1961	0.67
1960	1.48
1959	1.50
1958	1.76
1957	3.02
1956	2.86
1955	0.37

Chapter 9

Table 9.1 (Continued)
Consumer Price Index

Year	CPI
1954	-0.50
1953	0.63
1952	0.88

Source: *Business Conditions Digest* (June 1986), December to December Comparison.

Money Rate Risk

Money rate risk occurs when there are changes in the current interest rates. This risk can be seen especially in mortgage limited partnerships. For example, if a mortgage limited partnership's assets are comprised of long-term fixed rate mortgages, a rise in general interest rates would cause the value of a portfolio made up of existing loans to fall. Table 9.2 presents the interest rates on commitments of $100,000 and over for multiple and nonresidential mortgages.

Table 9.2
Commitments of $100,000 and Over on Multifamily and Nonresidential Mortgages
Commercial Mortgage Rates Made by Life Insurance Companies
(Average Interest Rates)

Year	Rate
1985	11.77
1984	12.88
1983	12.49
1982	14.36
1981	14.32
1980	12.62
1979	10.36
1978	9.59
1977	9.34
1976	9.83
1975	10.22

Source: American Council of Life Insurance. Table L.

The makeup of the loan portfolio in terms of its sensitivity to interest rate changes in general must also be examined. The interest payments may be based on either a fixed rate or a variable rate basis. To avoid the money rate risks, a mortgage limited partnership may require borrowers to assume the risk of rising interest rates through the use of variable rate financing.

ORGANIZATIONAL EXPENSES

Partnerships incur certain organizational costs relating to the forming of the limited partnership. These costs are amortized over a period of 60 months. Investors must be sure that these costs are reasonable based on the size of the offering. Under no circumstances should organization expenses exceed seven percent of the equity raised. For larger deals organizational expenses should be in the range of three to five percent.

SELLING COMMISSIONS

Mortgage limited partnership units are sold by registered representatives employed by brokerage firms. These individuals are compensated by the partnership for their selling efforts. Sales commissions, paid out of the proceeds of the offering, are usually under eight percent and are not deductible.

SHARING ARRANGEMENT

Sharing arrangements vary from program to program. Investors should require that they receive a preferential return of their initial contribution prior to any payout to the general partners. The general partners will in all likelihood require a yearly management fee. Additional compensation should be tied in to the performance of the limited partnership.

LIMITED PARTNER PAY-IN

Investment in a mortgage limited partnership may be comprised of a single pay-in. Investors must read the partnership agreement carefully to determine their pay-in requirements.

SUMMARY

Mortgage limited partnerships are formed to invest in either standard, insured, participating, or tax-exempt mortgages. Each of these limited partnerships has unique characteristics that depend on its objectives.

Since a mortgage limited partnership's primary source of income is interest income, it is important to compare the interest rates of the limited partnership's loan portfolio with those rates currently available in the marketplace. If, for example, the portfolio consists mostly of low-interest-rate loans, the value of the partnership will be adversely affected. Investors must also determine the loan's amortization period and evaluate the borrowers' ability to service the debt requirements.

In addition to the amount of debt, other terms of the loan are very important. Among these are the interest rate requirements and the repayment requirement. The interest rate on a debt instrument may be of either a fixed or a variable nature. Depending on the type, certain interest rate risks will be borne by either the lender or borrower. Some arrangements are of a participating nature, which entitles lenders to share in a predetermined amount of project profits in return for accepting a lower interest rate for their funds.

Mortgage limited partnerships have several advantages,

such as providing the small investor with professional management and diversification. On the other hand, investors in mortgage limited partnerships may be exposed to several risks. For mortgage limited partnerships that are uninsured, credit risks must be carefully evaluated. The risks of purchasing power reduction as well as money rate risks must be carefully evaluated especially when interest payments are of a fixed nature.

Chapter 10

Equipment Leasing
Limited Partnerships

Equipment leasing limited partnerships are formed for the purpose of acquiring equipment and leasing it to either corporate or noncorporate users. The leasee is able to use the equipment with leasing terms more beneficial an the outright purchase. The partnership passes on various tax benefits to the limited partners, who in turn provide the needed equity. In addition to yearly partial tax-free distributions, the limited partners are entitled to a stated percentage of the proceeds resulting from the sale of the equipment after the lease period.

GROWTH OF EQUIPMENT LEASING LIMITED PARTNERSHIPS

Since the Economic Recovery Act of 1981, equipment leasing limited partnerships have become increasingly popular as an investment device. Table 10.1 shows the total dollars invested in equipment limited partnerships from 1981 to 1985. The dollars invested in these partnerships tripled during this period.

The popularity of income-oriented equipment leasing limited partnerships is primarily attributed to their ability to provide high after-tax returns. This is accomplished through rapid depreciation write-offs over relatively short periods of time and the price received for the equipment at reversion.

Table 10.1
Dollars Invested in Equipment Leasing Partnerships

Year	Dollars invested
1985	$600,000,000*
1984	478,000,000
1983	386,500,000
1982	240,900,000
1981	200,000,000
* Estimated	

Source: *Stanger's Partnership Sponsor Directory.*

BUSINESS RISKS

Unlike real estate limited partnerships where the vacancy risks are sometimes quite high, possession of unleased assets is usually not a factor in equipment leasing programs. This is because equipment leasing limited partnerships will only acquire equipment after an agreement has been made with the user (leasee) of the equipment.

The success of a leasing program depends on the credit worthiness of the leasee. The financial strength of leasees is an important consideration in evaluating their credit quality. For the larger publicly-traded corporations, various sources of evaluation are available.

A proper assessment of the leasee's default risk will allow investors to avoid problems associated with having to release equipment and cover any debt payments in the meantime. A leasee's default could result in the lender foreclosing on the loan, exposing the equipment leasing limited partner to adverse tax consequences. In order to minimize these risks, investors should avoid programs where the leasee is relatively unknown and adequate credit information is unavailable.

RESIDUALS

The equipment's likely residual value must be determined next. The limited partnership memorandum should contain a residual appraisal of the property to be acquired. Not only does this give investors insight as to the sponsor's projections, but it also reinforces their expectations of earning profits (which they will need if questioned by the IRS). .

In many leasing deals, the forecast residual value of the equipment leased contributes most heavily to the investors' after-tax expected return. If, for example, the sponsors of an equipment leasing limited partnership incorrectly estimate the residual value to be equal to 80 percent of the original cost, when it turns out to be 20 percent, the after-tax return would decrease dramatically. Thus, the ability of the equipment to hold its value is the key to a successful equipment leasing program.

While tax deductions may enable investors to receive partial tax-free distributions during the leasing phase, the residual value of the equipment at the termination of the lease will ultimately determine whether the investment was worthwhile. In assessing the likely future residual value of leased equipment, investors must consider several items:

1. Prospects of technological obsolescence. Investors should study the history of the equipment type. Has the industry experienced rapid technological change? Are there any protective patents?

2. Viability of the company producing the equipment. If the manu-

facturer goes out of business, equipment owners may not be able to obtain spare or replacement parts. Furthermore, the value of manufacturer's warranties associated with the equipment would also be worthless in such an event.

The length of the initial lease term will provide significant insight as to the asset's likely residual value. Since equipment's residual value can be expected to diminish over time, the longer the lease period, the lower the residual value. Since equipment seldom holds its value or appreciates over time, the likelihood of capital gains is remote. Instead, the success of these investments depends on the likelihood of the residual being a fraction of the original cost.

FINANCING STRUCTURE

Income-oriented equipment leasing limited partnerships can range from programs totally financed by investors to programs that are moderately leveraged. In these latter types of partnerships, during the leasing phase, part of the rental income will be used to cover debt servicing requirements.

As stated earlier, the expected value of the residual is important in determining the amount of leverage available. The amount of leverage available to the partnership will increase as the residual value declines. This is because the leasee must pay the leasor more in rentals to compensate investors for the lower residual profits. Since the investors' borrowing capacity is directly tied to the size of the leasing income stream, they will be able to borrow more in instances where the residual is low. Items characterized by rapid obsolescence may be acquired with as little as 20 percent down spread over several years, while equipment possessing a higher residual may require more equity capital.

In addition to the amount of leverage involved, investors

must examine the terms of the debt to determine whether it calls for a variable or a fixed rate of interest. Investors must compare the debt servicing requirements to the lease payment requirements. If the interest rates are variable, then investors are left fully exposed to increases in interest rates, in the event that lease payments cannot be increased.

Investors should also determine the amount of principal that will be outstanding at the end of the initial leasing period. To do this, one must compare the length of the initial lease period with the amortization period of the loan. If the term of the loan is considerably longer than the initial lease, the residual may not be sufficient to cover debt repayment. In highly leveraged equipment leasing limited partnerships, investors sometimes experience what is called phantom income. *Phantom income* arises when the partnership experiences taxable income yet is unable to distribute cash to the limited partners to meet this obligation since all of its cash is applied to its debt servicing requirements.

Phantom income is a typical problem associated with highly leveraged equipment leasing limited partnerships. After the depreciation charges are exhausted, investors are exposed to taxable income without having the cash necessary to satisfy their tax obligations.

THE MASTER LEASE

Typically, equipment leasing limited partnerships will employ a master lease structure. Under this structure, the general partners will enter into a leasing arrangement (master lease) with the limited partners, whereby the general partners agree to be responsible for the contractual lease payments. The general partners then sublease the equipment to the user for a period of time shorter than the master lease.

MANAGEMENT FEES

Fees during the acquisition and operating period should be quite low compared to real estate limited partnerships. Equipment leasing is less involved and the general partners should receive little compensation during this period. In many equipment leasing limited partnerships, the general partners receive asset acquisition fees in lieu of management fees during the leasing phase. Under no circumstances should these fees exceed three percent of the price of the equipment purchased.

SHARING ARRANGEMENT

Equipment leasing limited partnerships provide that the proceeds from the sale of equipment be distributed between the limited and general partners. The limited partners should insist on at least 80 percent of the distributive cash resulting from the equipment sales.

TAX CONSIDERATIONS

Most income-oriented equipment leasing limited partnerships offer investors partial tax-free income as a result of rapid depreciation deductions. Under the ACRS, equipment can be depreciated using accelerated method using the half-year convention, over a 3-year, 5-year, 7-year, 10-year, or 15-year period, depending on the property class. Under the ACRS, no depreciation can be taken on equipment in the year that it is sold. (Many equipment leasing limited partnerships were structured to provide investors with investment tax credit (ITC) in addition to depreciation. However, the passage of the 1986 Tax Reform Act eliminated investment tax credits.)

To enjoy the favorable tax attributes available from equipment leasing, investors must be able to demonstrate that they entered into the transaction with a reasonable expectation of profits (in addition to tax benefits) and did not enter into the investment merely to postpone taxes.

A recent tax court ruling, commonly known as the E. F. Hutton decision, enhanced the attractiveness of equipment leasing limited partnerships. In that case, the court determined that even though the investors did not receive any cash distributions from the investment, a reasonable profit existed based on the sale of the equipment after the expiration of the lease. Since the reasonableness of the expected residual value of equipment is crucial to the profit motive, equipment leasing limited partnerships are basing their residual estimates more and more on evaluations by independent expert equipment appraisers.

In addition to attacking the profit motive of equipment leasing limited partnerships, the IRS may also challenge their claim to ownership of the equipment. Increasingly, the IRS has contended that these partnerships are financing arrangements and that the leasee, not the investor, is the true owner of the property. If the IRS is successful in this contention then the tax benefits of ownership (depreciation) would be disallowed.

In ruling on the ownership contention, the courts consider several factors. For example, they will determine whether the equipment was acquired at a fair market value and whether the rental income is at current market rates. This is why investors must be sure that the partnership meet these requirements by obtaining an appraisal from a reputable equipment appraisal firm.

Exposure to the Alternative Minimum Tax

While income-oriented equipment leasing programs may appear to be quite attractive, investors must consider the impact of these benefits as they relate to their own situations. Under the ACRS, accelerated depreciation of equipment is an item of tax preference. Thus investors sometimes find, after entering into such an arrangement, that their expected tax benefits do not materialize due to the alternate minimum tax.

Investment Interest Expense Limitation

Substantial deductions are available in highly leveraged equipment leasing limited partnerships. However, to the extent that they are the result of interest deductions, they may be of limited value. Investors must consider their own tax status when contemplating investing in an equipment leasing limited partnership.

In chapter 2, we discussed the investment interest expense limitation. The partnership will usually disclose the expected investment interest expense per individual limited partner.

At-Risk Provisions

IRS at-risk rules limit the amount of limited partners' passive loss deductions to their capital contribution and their pro rata share of partnership's recourse debt.

EQUIPMENT LEASING ILLUSTRATION

To demonstrate the concept of an equipment leasing arrangement, we will consider an investment in a hypothetical equipment leasing limited partnership. The assumptions underlying the leasing partnership are presented in table 10.2.

Table 10.2
Equipment Leasing Limited Partnership Assumptions
(200 Limited Partnership Units at $28,063 per unit

Total equity raised	$5,612,500
Cost of equipment purchased	5,000,000
Securities commissions	500,000
Organizational expenses (amortized over 60 months)	112,500
Residual value (year 6)	4,500,000
Operating expenses (as a percent of revenue)	15%
Limited partner's tax bracket	28%
Limited partners' share of profits (losses)	99%
General partners' share of profits (losses)	1%
Limited partners' share of cash distributions	99%
General partners' share of cash distributions	1%
Limited partners' share of residual cash flow	99%
General partners' share of residual cash flow	1%

PROFIT AND LOSS STATEMENTS

Table 10.3 presents the partnerships' forecast profit (loss) statements from years one through six based on the information contained in table 10.2. The assumptions underlying the forecast profit and loss statements are given in the following paragraph.

Revenue is forecast to be $1,275,000 during years one through six. Organizational expenses of $112,500 are amortized over the first five years at an annual rate of $22,500. Operating expenses represent 15 percent of rental income. The partnership's profit represents rental income less the sum of organizational, operating, interest, and depreciation expenses. The partnership's tax liability can be found by multiplying the yearly profits by 28 percent. The limited partners' tax liability is equal to 99 percent of the total partnership tax liability and can be found on the last line of table 10.3.

Chapter 10

Table 10.3
Profit (Loss) Statement
(28 percent tax bracket)

Year	1	2	3
Lease payments	$1,500,000	$1,500,000	$1,500,000
Less:			
Organizational expsenses	22,500	22,500	22,500
Operating expenses	225,000	225,000	225,000
Depreciation expenses	1,000,000	1,000,000	1,000,000
Profit	$ 252,500	$ 252,500	$ 252,500
Total tax liability	70,700	70,700	70,700
L.P. tax liability	$ 69,993	$ 69,993	$ 69,993

Year	4	5	6
Lease payments	$ 1,500,000	$ 1,500,000	$ 1,500,000
Less:			
Organizational expenses	22,500	22,500	0
Operating expenses	225,000	225,000	225,000
Depreciation expenses	1,000,000	1,000,000	0
Profit	$ 252,500	$ 252,500	$ 1,275,000
Total tax liability	70,700	70,700	357,000
L.P. tax liability	$ 69,993	$ 69,993	$ 353,430

Table 10.4
Yearly Tax Liability
(28 percent tax bracket)

Year	Initial outlay	Tax liability
0	($28,063)	-
1		$ 350
2		350
3		350
4		350
5		350
6		1,767
	($28,063)	$ 3,517

Table 10.4 shows the limited partners' tax liability based on their initial contribution of $28,063 ($5,612,500/200).

CASH FLOW STATEMENTS

Table 10.5 represents the partnership's forecast cash flows over a six-year period. The partnership's cash flow equals rental income less the sum of operating expenses. The limited partners' share equals 99 percent of the total cash available for distribution by the partnership. As a result of tax benefits, the limited partners receive cash distributions during the investment period.

Table 10.5
Cash Flow Statement

Year	1	2	3
Lease payments	$ 1,500,000	$ 1,500,000	$ 1,500,000
Less:			
Operating expenses	225,000	225,000	225,000
Cash flow	$ 1,275,000	$ 1,275,000	$ 1,275,000
L.P. cash flow	$ 1,262,250	$ 1,262,250	$ 1,262,250

Year	4	5	6
Lease payments	$ 1,500,000	$ 1,500,000	$ 1,500,000
Less:			
Operating expenses	225,000	225,000	225,000
Cash flow	$ 1,275,000	$ 1,275,000	$ 1,275,000
L.P. cash flow	$ 1,262,250	$ 1,262,250	$ 1,262,250

Table 10.6 reveals that an initial investment by the limited partner of $28,063 results in cash distributions totaling $37,866 during the initial six-year period.

Table 10.6
Yearly Cash Flow

Year	Initial investment	Cash flow
1	($28,063)	$ 6,311
2		6,311
3		6,311
4		6,311
5		6,311
6		6,311
TOTALS	($28,063)	$37,866

CASH DISTRIBUTIONS: RESIDUAL

In addition to the cash distributions during the leasing phase of the investment, the limited partners are also entitled to 99 percent of the proceeds from the sale of the equipment. Table 10.7 calculates the before-tax reversion assuming the equipment is sold at the end of year six, and that the residual value represents 90 percent of its original cost.

Table 10.7
Before-Tax Reversion

Sale price	$4,500,000
Limited partners cash distribution (99%)	4,455,000
Per limited partner	$ 22,275

Each individual limited partner would receive $22,275 ($4,455,000 / 200) at the time the asset is sold. However, individual investors must still pay taxes based on this distribution and their own adjusted basis.

PARTNERS' BASIS

Determining the limited partners' basis is important because the extent of each partner's tax liability at the time the asset is sold, is a function of the adjusted basis of his or her interest.

Although each limited partner's original basis is equal to his or her capital contribution plus the prorated share of the partnership liabilities, the basis for tax considerations may not be the same.

In addition to the passive loss provisions described in chapter 1, at-risk rules limit the amount of losses that individual investors can deduct relative to the amount they contribute and/or is personally liable for. Hence, if the investment involves borrowed funds, the debt must be of a recourse nature (that is, the investors must be personally liable for the debt's repayment) in order for the investors to be at risk.

In addition to capital contribution, a partner's basis can be increased through either taxable income of the partnership or increased borrowing by the partnership. The basis can be reduced through deductible partnership losses, distributions to the partner of partnership property, or reduction in the amount of partnership debt.

Table 10.8 demonstrates the calculation of a limited partner's capital account. The partner's basis is found by adding his or her share of the partnerships' profits less any cash distributions from initial contributions. Based on the calculations shown in table 10.8, the limited partner's adjusted basis is $2,756.

Table 10.8
Limited Partner's Adjusted Capital Account

(1) Year	(2) Equity investment	(3) Profit (losses)	(4) Cash distribution	(5) (2 + 3 -4) Adjusted basis
1	$28,063	$ 1,250	$6,311	
2	1,250	6,311		
3	1,250	6,311		
4	1,250	6,311		
5	1,250	6,311		
6	6,311	6,311		
TOTALS	$28,063	$ 12,561	$37,866	$ 2,756

Table 10.9 presents the after-tax reversion per limited partner. Since the limited partner's capital account is positive, partners must subtract their basis from that amount to their cash distribution to arrive at their profits on sale of the equipment.

Table 10.9
After-Tax Reversion per Limited Partner

Cash distribution	$ 22,275
Less:	
Adjusted basis of limited partner	2,756
Gain on sale	$ 19,519
Total liability (28% of gain on sale price)	5,465
After-tax reversion per limited partner	$ 16,810

In this example, each limited partner receives $22,275 before taxes from the sale of the equipment. Their total taxable profit is calculated to be $19,519 ($22,275 - $2,756). This profit would then be subject to tax at their marginal rate of 28 percent. Thus, they would pay taxes of $5,465. This would result in an after-tax reversion per limited partner of $16,810 ($22,275 – $5,465).

Table 10.10 summarizes the components of the limited partners' after-tax return. Now that we have identified the limited partners' expected tax liability, cash distribution, and after-tax reversion, we can calculate their after-tax return.

Using the tools developed in chapter 4, investors can now calculate their after-tax returns. The investors' after-tax return or internal rate of return (IRR) is calculated to be 16.24%, while the net present value (at 10 percent) is $5,989. Remember that these indicators of return are based on an assumed residual value of 90 percent.

Table 10.10
Limited Partner Return
($28,063 per unit)

Year	Sum invested	Tax liability	Cash flows	Due at reversion	Cumulative amounts
0	($28,063)				($28,063)
1		$ 350	$6,311		5,961
2		350	6,311		5,961
3		350	6,311		5,961
4		350	6,311		5,961
5		350	6,311		5,961
6		1,767	6,311	$16,810	21,354
TOTAL					$23,096

IRR = 16.24%
NPV(10%) = $5,989

RESIDUAL VALUE ASSUMPTIONS

Investors must carefully weigh the likelihood of this 90 percent residual value. If the residual value is less than 90 percent of the equipment's original cost, then the after-tax return will fall accordingly. Realization of a lower residual may leave investors with a sizable tax bill and no cash. In fact, if the residual is lower than the remaining balance of debt, they would be liable for the difference.

Table 10.11 illustrates the impact of various residual values on investors' after-tax reversion, net present value (discounted at 10 percent), and internal rate of return. As shown in table 10.11, varying the assumed residual value significantly affects investors' after-tax reversions, resulting in lower returns. A residual value of 25 percent of the equipment's original cost is necessary in order to realize a slight positive net present value of $45. At a residual value of 20 percent an investor would only have a 9.47 after-tax return on investment.

In fact, if the residual value turns out to be only 20 percent of the asset's original cost instead of the forecast 90 percent, the investment would provide a net present value of -$413. Thus in this particular limited partnership, the ability of the equipment to hold its value will determine the investment's profitability.

Table 10.11
Impact of Residual Assumptions
($5,000,000 original cost)

Assumed residual	After-tax reversion	Net present value (10%)	Internal rate return
90%	$16,810	$5,989	16.24%
85	15,919	5,531	15.84
80	15,028	5,074	15.42
75	14,137	4,617	14.99
70	13,246	4,160	14.56
65	12,355	3,702	14.11
60	11,464	3,245	13.65
55	10,573	2,788	13.18
50	9,682	2,331	12.70
45	8,791	1,874	12.20
40	7,900	1,416	11.69
35	7,009	959	11.16
30	6,118	502	10.62
25	5,227	45	10.06
20	4,336	- 413	9.47
15	3,445	- 870	8.87
10	2,554	1,327	8.24
5	1,663	-1,784	7.59

SUMMARY

Equipment leasing limited partnerships offer the investor partial tax-free distributions due to rapid depreciation deductions. The major economic risk facing investors in equipment leasing limited partnerships is the credit quality of the leasee. If leasees default on their payments, the equipment would be foreclosed upon, exposing investors to adverse tax consequences.

The ultimate success of an equipment leasing limited partnership is based on the realization of profits resulting from the sale of the equipment after the leasing phase of the investment period. Investors must therefore carefully consider the affects of inflation and obsolescence in determining whether the forecast residual value is reasonable.

Chapter 11

Oil And Gas Limited Partnerships

Oil and gas limited partnerships are formed to provide capital for oil exploration and/or development. These partnerships are structured so that the limited partners receive sizable first-year tax deductions and possible partially tax-free cash distributions when oil wells enter their productive stage.

Investors in oil and gas limited partnerships fared well in the early and mid-1970s as shortages lead to skyrocketing prices. However, the subsequent increase in worldwide supply and the reduction of worldwide consumption have sent oil and gas prices plummeting into the single-digit range for the first time in over 15 years.

The risks associated with these programs can be quite high. For example, people who invested in these partnerships in the later 1970s experienced unparallelled increases in the costs of financing, resulting in a minimal return on their investment. The U.S. government has provided various tax incentive programs in order to encourage exploration and development.

Table 11.1 provides a breakdown of the dollars invested in oil and gas limited partnerships based on public and private offerings for years 1984 and 1985. Recently, investments in oil and gas limited partnerships have been down overall. The total amount of capital raised in the partnership market declined by over 32 percent from 1984 to 1985. Private placement programs experienced a decline of 74.31 percent during this same period, while participation in public programs increased by 9.56 percent over this same period.

Table 11.1
Oil and Gas Partnership Market
($ in Millions)

Year	1984	1985	Percent change
Public	$1,694	$1,856	+9.56%
Private	1,674	430	-74.31%
TOTAL	$3,368	$2,286	-32.13%

Source: "Limited Partnership Sales Summary," *The Stanger Review* (1985), p. 1.

TYPES OF PROGRAMS

There are various types of oil and gas limited partnerships available to the public today. These partnerships can be categorized as follows: drilling, income, royalty/completion, combination, or master limited partnerships. Each of these oil and gas limited partnerships differs from the others in terms of return and risk. Table 11.2 presents a breakdown of the types of oil and gas partnerships and the corresponding capital raised.

Table 11.2
Sales of Publicly Registered Limited Partnerships

	1984	1985	Percent change 1984-1985
Drilling	$ 414.3	$ 370.7	-10.5%
Income	985.5	253.7	-74.3
Royalty/completion	63.8	72.7	14.0
Combination	19.0	0.0	-100.0
Master limited partnership	211.5	1,159.4	448.2
TOTAL	$1,694.1	$1,856.5	9.1%

Source: "Limited Partnership Sales Summary," *The Stanger Review* (1985).

Drilling Programs

These limited partnership programs can involve drilling in areas where oil and gas reserves are known (*proven reserves*) or in areas adjacent to proven reserves (*stepout drilling*). Developmental programs that involve drilling in areas of known reserves contain relatively few risks.

Exploratory drilling or "wildcat drilling," on the other hand, involves a great deal of risk. It involves exploration in areas of unknown or unproven reserves. As many as 80 percent or more of all wildcat wells drilled are failures. Exploratory drilling also occurs in areas where there are proven reserves but not at the depth targeted. These deep-test drilling programs also involve a great deal of risk.

Thus, oil and gas limited partnerships offer a range of drilling programs ranging from exploratory to development drilling. In addition, "balanced" drilling partnerships provide the investor with diversification by allocating expenditures between exploratory and development drilling. Investors' choices depend on their own return and risk preferences. Table 11.2 shows that total capital raised by drilling limited partnerships declined in 1985 by approximately 10.5 percent from 1984.

Income Programs

Income programs are formed for the purpose of acquiring the rights to extract oil and/or gas (called "working interest") of existing properties producing oil and gas. The risks associated with exploration can be avoided in this type of program. Cash flows under these programs are more predictable (as compared to exploratory drilling). As shown in table 11.2, the total capital raised in 1985 by income programs dropped by over 74 percent from its 1984 level, mainly due to the decline in oil prices.

Combination Programs

These oil and gas limited partnerships engage in drilling operations and the purchasing of properties already producing oil and gas. Such programs offer less risk than is found in a typical drilling program, since part of their expenditures are earmarked for existing properties. As shown in table 11.2, there were no new public combination programs registered during 1985.

Royalty/Completion Programs

Royalty oil and gas limited partnerships engage in the acquisition of royalties. These programs purchase mineral rights, overriding royalties, and "nonparticipating" oil and gas royalties. Completion programs are designed only to fund the capital cost of equipment involved in drilling, and oil and gas production. These programs increased by over 14 percent in 1985 over 1984.

Master Limited Partnerships

The master limited partnership is the most rapidly growing oil and gas limited partnership available today. Between 1984 and 1985 sales of these publicly registered partnerships increased by over 400 percent. Typically, the master limited partnership is formed by acquiring the interest of existing oil and gas exploration programs whose value is determined by independent hydrocarbon engineers. Cash generated from these investments can either be reinvested into other existing oil and gas exploration programs or paid out to investors at the discretion of the general partners.

The master limited partnership, a relative new innovation, provides investors with liquidity by allowing them to trade their oil and gas interest in the secondary market. Investors are able to take advantage of the tax benefits associated with oil and gas limited partnerships without being at the mercy of the general partners in terms of disposal of their partnership interest. Thus, the master limited partnership avoids the major pitfall of other types of limited partnerships, that is, the lack of liquidity.

Table 11.3 provides a list of oil and gas master limited partnerships that are traded on the New York Stock Exchange, American Stock Exchange, or the over-the-counter market. Master limited partnership units are traded on a daily basis, providing investors with information as to the current market value of their interest.

Table 11.3
Oil and Gas
Master Limited Partnerships
(Traded Publicly)

Program name	Market
Apache Petroleum Company	NYSE
Belden & Blake Energy Company	AMEX
ConVest Energy Partners, Ltd.	AMEX
Damson Energy-A	AMEX
Damson Energy-B	AMEX
Diamond Shamrock Offshore Partners	NYSE
Dorchester Hugoton, Ltd.	OTC
Enserch Exploration Partners, Ltd.	NYSE
Entex Energy Development, Ltd.	NYSE
Freeport-McMoRan Energy Partners, Ltd.	NYSE
Graham-McCormick Oil and Gas Partnership	AMEX
Great American Partners	OTC
Lear Petroleum Partners, L.P.	AMEX
May Energy Partners	AMEX
Newhall Resources, Ltd.	NYSE
NRM Energy Company, L.P.	AMEX
OKC Limited Partnership	OTC
Petroleum Investments. Ltd.	NYSE
Snyder Oil Partners	NYSE
Transco Exploration Partners, Ltd.	NYSE
Union Exploration Partners, Ltd.	NYSE

REVENUE ANALYSIS

Revenues from an oil and gas program are influenced by the productive capacity of the wells as well as the price received from the fuel extracted. Investors in oil and gas limited partnerships can be exposed to rapidly changing prices as evidenced by the oil price declines experienced by the oil industry in early 1986. As shown in table 11.4, the price of crude oil increased steadily during the 1970s and early 1980s only to plummet as a result of overproduction and a decrease in world-wide demand.

Table 11.4
Average Price per Barrel of Crude Oil
(Rotterdam)

Year	World spot price
1986	$11.56
1985	24.00
1984	28.41
1983	30.39
1982	34.00
1981	32.88
1980	26.00
1979	13.34
1978	12.70
1977	12.09
1976	11.51
1975	10.46
1974	9.60
1973	2.10
1972	1.90
1971	1.75
1970	1.35

Source: "Annual Energy Outlook 1985," *Monthly Energy Review* (DOE/EIA-0035), Energy Information Administration, p.53.

Table 11.5 shows the world oil consumption pattern. The United States is responsible for over a quarter of the world's total oil consumption. Western Europe consumes an additional 20 percent of that total. The Middle East accounts for only three percent of worldwide consumption.

Table 11.5
World Oil Consumption

Location	Percentage of consumption
United States	26.1%
Western Europe	20.9
Western Hemisphere	10.2
Asia	14.2
Communist Nations	22.7
Middle East	3.0
Africa	2.9
TOTAL	100.0

Source: *Petroleum Supply Annual*, Energy Information Association, June 1986, p. 66.

The consumption patterns become more significant when compared to the location of existing world oil reserves. Table 11.6 presents a breakdown of the world oil reserves. The Organization of Petroleum Exporting Countries (OPEC) controls over 60 percent of the known oil reserves, whereas the United States controls only 4 percent. Both the U.S.S.R. and Mexico control considerably more oil reserves than does the United States. This imbalance between U.S. consumption (26.1%) and reserves (4.0%) suggests that the United States will probably continue to be dependent on oil imports for the foreseeable future. This also suggests that prices will continue to fluctuate based on supply-and-demand considerations.

Historically, the natural gas industry has been heavily regulated. This has created imbalances between supply and demand, resulting in overpriced gas. The deregulation of this industry should move a long way in correcting this problem.

The Federal Energy Regulatory Commissions' Order 436 allows end users to purchase natural gas at the wellhead directly, rather than from the pipeline companies. Thus, the end users are in touch with the producers and lower transmission costs result from the increased competition among pipeline companies.

Table 11.6
World Oil Reserves

Location	Percentage of known reserves
OPEC	62.2%
U.S.S.R.	9.8
Mexico	7.2
United States	4.0
China	2.9
Others	13.9
TOTAL	100.0

Source: *Petroleum Supply Annual*, Energy Information Association, June 1986, p. 65.

ROYALTY

Oil and gas limited partnership programs acquire rights to produce from either the land owner or mineral owners by entering into a lease agreement. In consideration for the right to produce oil and gas, the lessor will be given a percentage of the production from the extraction of the oil and gas. This is called an overriding royalty interest, which entitles the lessor to a specified fraction of the production free of any production or operating expenses, and thus is said to be "nonparticipating." However, it is not free from production or severance taxes.[1]

[1] *The Stanger Register*, Volume IV, number 10, October 1985, page 144.

ACQUISITION EXPENSES

The expenses involved in oil and gas programs include lease-hold acquisition costs. The leasehold acquisition costs represent any costs associated with acquiring the working interest of a property. A working interest is "the right in an oil or gas leasehold which is subject to any portion of the expense of development, operation, or maintenance."[2] This would include geological reports, legal fees, fees paid to the landowners or mineral owners, and fees paid to brokers for securing the lease. These costs must be capitalized for income tax purposes.

INTANGIBLE DRILLING AND DEVELOPMENT COSTS

Intangible costs are comprised of noncapital drilling and development expenses incurred by the limited partnership. These costs include expenditures for site preparation, drilling, supplies, workers, fuel, and all other noncapital costs which are normally incurred in drilling and development.

Drilling costs, measured on a per foot basis, have declined somewhat from their high in 1982. (Table 11.7 presents the average on-shore drilling costs from the late 1960s to present.) Many drilling programs enter into turnkey contracts, where the driller agrees to drill for a particular price. The risk of drilling is then transferred to the drilling entity for a mutually agreeable price.

MANAGEMENT FEES

Many oil and gas limited partnerships specify that a certain percentage of fees be paid out of the capital proceeds, while an

[2]Ibid.

Table 11.7
Average On-Shore Drilling Costs

Year	Drilling cost per foot
1984	$71.90
1983	83.34
1982	108.73
1981	80.63
1980	66.86
1979	58.29
1978	49.72
1977	41.16
1976	37.35
1975	34.17
1974	27.82
1973	22.54
1972	20.77
1971	18.41
1970	19.29
1969	19.28
1968	18.63

Source: *Oil and Gas Journal* (December 17, 1984), p.41.

additional amount be paid from the project's revenues. The general partners may receive a first-year management fee as well as a supervisory fee based on the number of producing wells. In any event, investors should try to maximize the amount of their capital invested in the project itself.

Investors must identify partnerships which provide them with the greatest possibility of success. A key indicator of success is the "percent in ground." The percent in ground refers to the percentage of the limited partners' capital contribution that actually goes into the planned activity itself. As a rule of thumb, investors should shy away from deals where the percent in ground is less than 85 percent. Thus, a percent in ground equalling 85 would indicate that 15 percent of the limited partners' capital is being allocated to cover such expenses as selling commissions, organizational costs, acquisition costs, and other general partner' fees. The more capital put into the ground, the greater the expected profitability.

MANAGEMENT'S TRACK RECORD

The oil and gas limited partnership prospectus provides information regarding the general partners' past business experience. Although evaluating a successful past cannot guarantee a profitable future, it can be a useful screening tool when deciding on purchasing limited partnership interest. Investors should avoid offerings where the general partners are not seasoned participants.

TAX CONSIDERATIONS

Typically, limited partnerships allocate all of the intangible drilling and development expenses to the limited partner. This tax advantage is extremely important because intangible drilling and development expenses usually represent a significant portion of the partnership's initial expenditures. Since a substantial portion of these costs may be deducted in the year that they are incurred, investors in oil and gas limited partnerships may write off as much as 60 percent or more of their initial investment during the first year.

In addition to the intangible drilling and development costs, limited partners may also be entitled to a depletion deduction from income resulting from removal and sale of oil and gas. The depletion allowance enacted by Congress allows the producer to write off a portion of the depleted substance. For independent producers who are engaged in exploration of unproven reserve areas, the percentage depletion method is available. Under this depletion method a percentage of revenue (currently 15 percent) can be written off.

Alternative Minimum Tax

Oil and gas limited partnerships sometimes expose investors to the alternative minimum tax. Investors are required to treat excess intangible drilling costs as tax preference items. If these costs are capitalized, investors may avoid the alternative minimum tax. The alternative minimum tax does not apply for wells that are nonproductive. Investors must evaluate the program based on their own individual circumstances.

Investment Interest Expense Limitation

Investors should determine the yearly amount of investment interest expense per limited partnership unit. Investors are limited as to the amount of investment interest expense they can deduct in any one tax year. Investors must consider the impact of the investment interest expense limitation as it relates to their personal situations.

At-Risk Provisions

Oil and gas limited partnership investments are subject to the at-risk provisions, which place a limit on the amount that can be deducted equal to the investors' capital contribution and their share of the partnership's recourse debt. Even though individuals who own oil and gas working interest can use partnership losses to offset ordinary income, they are still subject to the at-risk provisions of the tax code. Thus, those who invest in oil and gas limited partnerships and receive deductions in excess of their cash contributions must be at risk for that excess.

ORGANIZATIONAL EXPENSES

The partnership incurs costs associated with the organization of the partnership itself. Total front-end expenses, including organizational expenses, should not exceed 15 percent of the capital raised.

SELLING COMMISSIONS

Oil and gas limited partnership interests are usually sold by registered representatives employed by a brokerage firm. Sales commission, paid out of the proceeds of the offering, averages six to eight percent of the proceeds. Sales commissions sometimes equal ten percent or more.

SHARING ARRANGEMENT

The sharing arrangement is determined by the type of program being offered. Many oil and gas drilling programs allocate the entire intangible drilling costs to the limited partners. The general partners who own the necessary equipment are then responsible for the costs associated with its maintenance and replacement.

Table 11.8 lists the items of allocation between the limited and general partners. The percentages associated with each category are influenced by the type of program, the relative contributions of participants (limited and general partners),

and other compensation arrangements (such as general partners' fees).

Table 11.8
Allocation of Partnership Items

Items	Limited partners	General partners
REVENUES:		
Revenues from sale of oil and gas	%	%
Salvage value of capital equipment	%	%
Farmout proceeds	%	%
EXPENSES:		
Organization expenses	%	%
Management fees	%	%
Intangible drilling costs	%	%
Capital costs	%	%
Operating costs	%	%
General and administrative overhead	%	%

PARTNER PAY-IN

Some oil and gas limited partnerships require a single pay-in;
others require installments over a period of time. By spreading the payment over a period of years, limited partnerships
can increase their yearly write-offs. In addition to the capital
contribution, many oil and gas limited partnerships impose
assessments on the limited partners based on a percentage of
their initial capital contribution.

The partnership may also require that individual investors
become personally liable for the debts of the partnership.
While recourse financing increases investors' capacity for
write-offs, it also increases their exposure to risks.

Chapter 11

SUMMARY

Oil and gas limited partnerships may engage in a wide range of activities, such as drilling, income, royalty/completion, combination, and master limited partnership programs. These programs may be formed for the purpose of engaging in oil exploration, acquiring existing productive wells, or purchasing royalty interests. In addition, master limited partnerships provide much-needed liquidity by acquiring already-existing programs and enabling participants to sell their units on the organized stock exchange.

Under current law, intangible drilling and development expenditures may be written off as incurred rather than being capitalized, thus providing investors with sizable deductions. A depletion allowance is also available to investors. These deductions may be calculated as a percentage of the investors' capital investment in the partnership's property. In some instances, the partners can elect to use the more attractive percentage depletion method.

Intangible drilling and development costs are an item of tax preference and may limit the amount of taxes that can be delayed. The individual investor must carefully evaluate the impact of the alternative minimum tax, since the investor's particular situation will determine the usefulness of such investments.

Chapter 12

Research And Development Limited Partnerships

Research and development limited partnerships provide funds for entities to explore and develop new and unproven products, in return for the right to share in the profits resulting from the new technology. These limited partnership are becoming an increasingly popular means of funding high-risk ventures that require sizable up-front financing while providing investors with the opportunity sharing a significant portion of the venture's profits.

The total research and development market in the United States increased by over 41 percent from 1984 to 1985. As table 12.1 shows, the greatest percentage increase was in public research and development programs, which increased by 60.8 percent. However, the largest dollar concentration was in private research and development programs. Private research and development programs accounted for over 84 percent ($850,000,000/$1,009,000,000) of the total dollars invested in R&D partnerships.

Table 12.1
Research and Development Venture Capital
Total Partnership Market
($ in millions)

Program type	1984	1985	Percentage change 1984-1985
Public	$ 99	$ 159	60.8%
Private	615	850	38.3%
TOTAL	$714	$1,009	41.4%

Source: "Limited Partnership Sales Summary 1985," *The Stanger Review*, p. 1.

INVESTMENT PROGRAMS

Research and development limited partnerships invest in a wide range of industries. These programs can be involved in activities such as genetic engineering, computer technology, communications, data processing, as well as other high-tech activities. Research and development limited partnerships often engage in joint ventures with well-known, established companies.

INVESTMENT RISKS

These investments typically expose investors to substantial amounts of business and financial risk. The nature of research is such that there exists significantly more risk than an investment in a known technology or product. Furthermore, it may be years before the new technology enters the marketplace and many more years before it becomes profitable. To

illustrate this concept, figure 12.1 presents the typical product
life cycle.

As seen in figure 12.1, the product life cycle consist of four
stages: pioneering, expansion, stabilization, and decline. The
first stage is highlighted by a technological innovation that
requires large research-related expenditures and usually results in losses. During the expansion stage, the firm is able to
reduce its production costs (due to its learning curve) and
usually results in increasing profits. Then the product enters
the stabilization stage where profits begin to decrease as more
and more firms enter the market, often copying the innova-
tor's technology (reverse engineering) without infringing on
its patents. Eventually, the product enters the decline stage as

Figure 12.1
Product Life Cycle
(Stages)

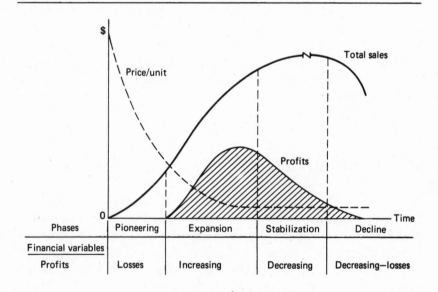

Phases	Pioneering	Expansion	Stabilization	Decline
Financial variables				
Profits	Losses	Increasing	Decreasing	Decreasing—losses

the market becomes saturated and/or other more advanced technologies compete for sales. At this stage, profits decrease and the product may even experience losses.

In the event that research leads to product development, the risk of technological obsolescence can threaten the profitability of such profits. The rapid pace of technological change poses additional risks in markets where there is significant competition. The possibility of duplicating products through reverse engineering may result in profit shortfall even if research is successful.

Furthermore, additional money may be needed to fund continued research. The uncertainty surrounding new and unproven technology precludes an accurate determination of the total funds necessary for the completion of projects. If the partnership is unable to fund additional research, then the project may have to be abandoned.

While new technology may be attainable, the product may not be commercially viable due to factors such as high costs, or small markets. Often the commercial viability cannot be ascertained until a project is well into the research phase.

Finally, the integrity of the product may not be protected. The ability of the entity to obtain a patent or to maintain product/process trade secrets are important considerations in assessing investment risks.

DIVERSIFICATION

Since investment in research and development limited partnerships subjects investors to significant business and financial risks, it is imperative that the program selected provide investors with a well-diversified portfolio of investment opportunities. The ability of the limited partnership to invest in several ventures will reduce the overall risk of the partnership itself.

The potential profits from the development of one successful venture may be sufficient to offset the losses resulting from failure of other ventures.This concept of risk spreading is particularly important in research and development limited partnerships. The risks of failure are high enough without investors putting all their eggs in one basket. Therefore, proper diversification is the heart of successful research and development investing.

TAX CONSIDERATIONS

The attractiveness of research and development limited partnerships from a tax standpoint is based on the ability of the limited partners to deduct research or experimental expenditures as they are incurred, subject to the passive loss provisions of the code. Typically, such research expenditures are allocated to the limited partners in return for their capital contributions. However, these expenses must be "in connection with a trade or business."

Alternative Minimum Tax

The ability of investors to reduce their taxes through deductions associated with research or experimental expenditures may also be limited due by the alternative minimum tax provisions. The tax code treats up to 90 percent of these expenditures as tax preference items, and thus may be of little use to those investors who are subject to the alternative minimum tax. It is therefore important that individual investors understand fully their own individual tax circumstances before they enter into a research and development limited partnership.

Excess Investment Interest Expense Limitation

The investors' deductions may also be limited by the amount of investment interest expense they can deduct in any one year. If the partnership specifies that debt be used, investors should determine if any deductions resulting from its use will be limited due to this restriction.

ORGANIZATIONAL EXPENSES

The partnership will incur certain organizational costs relating to the forming of the limited partnership. These costs will be amortized over a period of 60 months. Investors must be sure that these costs are reasonable based on the size of the offering.

SELLING EXPENSES

Research and development limited partnership units are sold by registered representatives employed by brokerage firms. These people are compensated by the partnership for their selling efforts. Sales commissions, which are paid out of the proceeds of the offering, will range from six to ten percent and are not deductible.

SHARING ARRANGEMENT

Sharing arrangements vary from program to program. Investors should require that they receive a preferential return of their initial contribution prior to any payout to the general partners. The general partners will in all likelihood require a yearly management fee. Additional compensation should be tied in to the performance of the limited partnership.

LIMITED PARTNER PAY-IN

Investment in research and development limited partnerships may be comprised of a series of pay-ins or a single pay-in. In the latter instance, the partnership may require additional contributions to fund additional research if required. Investors must read the partnership agreement carefully to determine their pay-in requirements.

SUMMARY

Research and development limited partnerships involve a high amount of business and financial risk. Investing in new technologies involves a great deal more risk than an investment in a known and proven technology. Competition adds to the riskiness of these investments. The cornerstone of a well-structured research and development limited partnership is diversification. Since the prospects of any one venture succeeding are small, investors must diversify in order to spread their overall risk.

Investors in these limited partnerships are able to deduct research and experimental expenditures in the year they are incurred against other passive income. However, investors' deductions are limited to the amount they have at risk in the partnership. Furthermore, a substantial amount of these research and experimental expenditures are treated as tax preference items. Thus investors must carefully consider their own circumstances (in terms of the alternative minimum taxes) before investing in research and development limited partnerships.

Chapter 13

Exotic Limited Partnerships

In addition to the investments already examined, limited partnerships are also created to fund more exotic types of investments. Investors have the opportunity of participating in these less traditional types of investments that provide tax benefits as well as the possibility of achieving significant after-tax returns. Just as the potential returns can be quite attractive, so can the risks. Nevertheless, these investments are becoming increasingly popular as investment alternatives.

Investment in these publicly-registered exotic programs has increased faster than real estate, equipment leasing, oil and gas, or research and development public programs. Table 13.1 presents a summary of publicly-registered miscellaneous program sales for years 1984 and 1985. Investment in these limited partnerships grew by over 106.0 percent during this period.

Each of these limited partnership programs offers investors the potential of earning significant profits, while exposing them to a variety of risks, some of which are unique to the

Table 13.1
Publicly Registered Miscellaneous Program Sales Summary

($ in millions)

	1984	1985	Percentage change 1984-1985
Cable TV	87.2	183.4	110.3%
Commodities	48.6	78.4	61.3
Films	60.2	235.8	291.7
Agriculture/Livestock	89.1	309.3	247.1
Other	159.2	108.5	-31.7
TOTAL	$444.3	$ 915.4	106.0%

Source: "Partnership Sales Summary 1985," *The Stanger Review*, p. 2.

investment contemplated. Individual investors must evaluate each of these investments in terms of their reward/risk characteristics and their suitability to the individual's own special needs. While many of these investments may be unsuitable to most investors, they can nevertheless be appropriate given the circumstances of the individual investor.

CABLE TV

Cable TV limited partnerships are formed for the purpose of acquiring and managing cable television stations. Generally, these partnerships acquire an existing station with the objective of increasing profit margins and thus increasing the value of such acquisitions. Limited partners provide equity capital in return for potential future years tax-free cash distributions.

The number of subscribers to cable TV has increased dramatically since 1970. As shown in table 13.2, the number of

Table 13.2
Growth of Cable TV

Year	Operating systems	Total number of basic subscribers (thousands)
1985	6,800	38,000
1984	6,200	30,000
1983	5,600	25,000
1982	4,825	21,000
1981	4,375	18,300
1980	4,225	16,000
1979	4,150	14,100
1978	3,875	13,000
1977	3,832	11,900
1976	3,681	10,800
1975	3,506	9,800
1974	3,158	8,700
1973	2,991	7,300
1972	2,841	6,000
1971	2,639	5,300
1970	2,470	4,500

Source: *Television and Cable Fact Book 1985 Edition*, Television Digest Study for National Cable Television Association, p. 1735.

basic subscribers increased from 4,500,000 in 1970 to 38,000,000 in 1985. During that same period the number of operating systems increased from 2,470 (1970) to 6,800 (1985).

The Cable Communications Policy Act of 1984 redefines the regulatory authority of federal, state, and local governments. Under this act, the Federal Communications Commission is responsible for rules of ownership as well as other nonprogramming rules. Effective January 1, 1987, states and municipalities are no longer permitted to regulate prices of cable services.

Revenues from these investments are generated through advertising, subscriber payments, and circulation revenues. Often the limited partnership finances a significant portion of the overall investment to lever profits. These limited partnerships may also seek to reduce the TV station's cash operating costs to improve the prospects of a profitable disposal of the property.

The partnership acquires assets that can be depreciated over varying periods of time. Real property, such as nonresidential buildings, will be depreciated over a 31.5-year period, while equipment will be written off over a much shorter period. This enables the limited partnership to distribute to the investors cash which will be primarily tax-free.

Cable TV limited partnerships involve a high degree of business risk. The partnership's ability to increase and maintain profit margins will be through the use of a combination of revenue increases and cost-cutting measures. Rising programming costs, increased competition, and government regulation may adversely affect profits.

CATTLE BREEDING

Cattle breeding limited partnerships are formed to purchase, breed, milk, and sell cows. The partnership engages in culling the herd or removing inferior cows to insure successful breeding. The management of cattle herds requires an expert knowledge of feeding, culling, and selling cows. In addition, management must be knowledgeable in the marketing of embryos and semen, since these activities are crucial to the profitability of the operation.

Normal expenses associated with feeding, culling, marketing, and insurance can be passed on to limited partners in return for their capital contributions. In addition to these expenses, cows may also be eligible for depreciation. Breeding or dairy cows can be depreciated over a relatively small number of years, depending on when the cows are placed into service. However, cows intended for resale cannot be depreciated.

Among the risks associated with cattle breeding is a drop in productivity caused by death, disease, or sterility, as well as rising costs of feed and lack of appreciation of the herd. Furthermore, milk prices have a significant effect on the profitability of milk-producing cows.

HORSE SYNDICATIONS

While horse ownershp was once associated with royalty, today many individuals are choosing to invest in horses. Top-quality horses command ever increasing prices, as demand far outpaces supply. Investors can enjoy significant profits as well as attractive tax benefits by taking part in horse syndications. Expenses associated with boarding, feeding, marketing, and insurance can be used to offset any revenues realized in this activity.

Horses can be purchased for both racing and breeding purposes. In fact, the reproduction capability of these investments provide for unlimited profits.

Depending on bloodlines, breeding can produce significant cash flows to the partnership. Top-quality stallions command high prices in stud fees, while broodmares receive sizable bids for their offspring. Horses acquired for breeding purposes can be depreciated under the accelerated cost recovery system; however, offspring can not be depreciated for tax purposes.

The advantage of horse syndications is that these programs generally invest in several horses, thus providing investors with risk reduction through diversification. In addition, syndications involve general partners who are experts in the field and can identify top-quality horses. By pooling their money, individual investors may acquire horses beyond the finances of the average investor.

The most difficult aspect of investing in horse syndications is the determination of the horse's value. Since the earning potential of a Secretariat or a Native Dancer are so great, values can be quite high. However, few horses will provide these returns, and many investors have been disappointed.

ORANGE GROVES

Orange grove limited partnerships are formed to acquire, own, and operate orange groves. Limited partners contribute capital in return for partially tax-free cash distributions. The attractiveness of an investment in orange groves is due to the ability of citrus trees to produce fruit over asubstantial period of time, and thus provide investors with continued cash flow long after the tax deductions have ended.

Revenues are generated through the sale of oranges. Total revenues are determined by the property's yield per acre, the number of acres owned, the type of orange produced, and the price prevalent (for fresh and processed fruit) in the market. Increased foreign competition (especially from Brazil) may limit price increases.

Costs associated with orange production include grove maintenance, irrigation, picking and hauling of fruit, and marketing requirements.Orange trees are subject to depreciation under current law.

Orange grove limited partnerships are subject to a wide variety of risks in addition to volatile prices. For example, orange trees are subject to disease. Orange groves may have to be burned to avoid the canker disease. The Mediterranean fruit fly and other pests also threaten the health of trees. Furthermore, adverse weather conditions can be devastating. Freezing temperatures or lack of proper irrigation can cripple an orange grove crop.

Finally, the citrus industry is heavily dependent upon migrant workers for the picking of fruit. Changes in the work force due to government regulation or possible unionization of workers might cause profit margins to suffer. Investors must be willing to accept these risks if they choose to invest in orange grove limited partnerships.

MOTION PICTURES

Motion picture limited partnerships are formed for the purpose of participating in the production, ownership and distribution of motion pictures. Typically, these partnerships enter into joint venture arrangements with reputable firms in the motion picture industry. The limited partners provide equity capital in return for a negotiated percentage of the revenues from the film projects undertaken.

Although the potential return form these partnerships can be quite attractive, investors are also exposed to a high degree of business risk. The production, promotion, and distribution of motion pictures involves a substantial amount of up-front capital. The recovery of these expenditures is dependent upon motion picture's "success at the box office," as well as the producers' ability to stay within the budget.

Each limited partnership should be evaluated based on the proposed sharing arrangement, the track record of the coventurer, the participants in the film (cast, producers, and directors), and the theme of the film itself.

COMMODITIES

Commodity limited partnerships are formed to provide capital for the speculative trading in options, futures, and forward contracts for profits. These partnerships enable investors to engage in these activities with the services of knowledgeable experts. In addition, these partnerships provide investors with an otherwise unattainable level of diversification.

Trading in these markets involves a high degree of risk. Prices are volatile, and the transaction fees are quite high. Furthermore, the use of leverage can expose investors to sizable losses. These types of limited partnerships should only be contemplated by highly seasoned investors.

ADDITIONAL TAX CONSIDERATIONS

In addition to the risks already examined, investors must consider the exotic investment's impact on other tax areas. Some of the other important considerations are highlighted below.

Alternative Minimum Tax

Each investment must be evaluated in terms of the alternative minimum taxes. In addition to considering the risks already cited, investors must carefully evaluate the risk of increased tax exposure prior to investing in any of these partnerships. Failure to do so may result in substantially greater tax liabilities than expected.

Investment Interest Expense Limitation

Investors' deductions may also be limited by the amount of investment interest expense they can deduct in any one year. If the partnership specifies that debt be used, investors should determine if any deductions resulting from its use will be limited due to this restriction.

ORGANIZATIONAL EXPENSES

The partnership will incur certain organizational costs relating to the forming of the limited partnership. These costs will be amortized over a period of 60 months. Investors must be sure that these costs are reasonable.

SELLING COMMISSIONS

Exotic limited partnership units are sold by registered representatives employed by brokerage firms. These individuals are compensated by the partnership for their selling efforts. Sales commissions, paid out of the proceeds of the offering, will range from six to ten percent and are not deductible.

SHARING ARRANGEMENT

Sharing arrangements vary from program to program. Investors should require that they receive a preferential return of their initial contribution prior to any payout to the general partners. The general partner will in all likelihood require a yearly management fee. Additional compensation should be tied in to the performance of the limited partnership.

LIMITED PARTNER PAY-IN

Investment in exotic limited partnership may be comprised of a series of pay-ins or a single pay-in. Investors must read the partnership agreement carefully to determine their pay-in requirements.

Chapter 13

SUMMARY

Exotic limited partnerships offer investors a wide range of investment opportunities, each with its own potential for substantial returns. They also may expose investors to risks significantly greater than those likely under more traditional limited partnership investments.

Exotic investments such as cable TV, films, commodities, cattle breeding, horse syndications, and orange groves are available through securities dealers and must be evaluated on their own merits. Investors must consider the investment's impact on their alternative minimum taxes, investment interest limitations, and any future capital requirements.

Appendix A

Compound of $1

Period	1%	2%	3%	4%	5%	6%	7%	8%	9%	10%
1	1.0100	1.0200	1.0300	1.0400	1.0500	1.0600	1.0700	1.0800	1.0900	1.1000
2	1.0201	1.0404	1.0609	1.0816	1.1025	1.1236	1.1449	1.1664	1.1881	1.2100
3	1.0303	1.0612	1.0927	1.1249	1.1576	1.1910	1.2250	1.2597	1.2950	1.3310
4	1.0406	1.0824	1.1255	1.1699	1.2155	1.2625	1.3108	1.3605	1.4116	1.4641
5	1.0510	1.1041	1.1593	1.2167	1.2763	1.3382	1.4026	1.4693	1.5386	1.6105
6	1.0615	1.1262	1.1941	1.2653	1.3401	1.4185	1.5007	1.5869	1.6771	1.7716
7	1.0721	1.1487	1.2299	1.3159	1.4071	1.5036	1.6058	1.7138	1.8280	1.9487
8	1.0829	1.1717	1.2668	1.3686	1.4775	1.5938	1.7182	1.8509	1.9926	2.1436
9	1.0937	1.1951	1.3048	1.4233	1.5513	1.6895	1.8385	1.9990	2.1719	2.3579
10	1.1046	1.2190	1.3439	1.4802	1.6289	1.7908	1.9672	2.1589	2.3674	2.5937
11	1.1157	1.2434	1.3842	1.5395	1.7103	1.8983	2.1049	2.3316	2.5804	2.8531
12	1.1268	1.2682	1.4258	1.6010	1.7959	2.0122	2.2522	2.5182	2.8127	3.1384
13	1.1381	1.2936	1.4685	1.6651	1.8856	2.1329	2.4098	2.7196	3.0658	3.4523
14	1.1495	1.3195	1.5126	1.7317	1.9799	2.2609	2.5785	2.9372	3.3417	3.7975
15	1.1610	1.3459	1.5580	1.8009	2.0789	2.3966	2.7590	3.1722	3.6425	4.1772

Appendix A

Period	1%	2%	3%	4%	5%	6%	7%	8%	9%	10%
16	1.1726	1.3728	1.6047	1.8730	2.1829	2.5404	2.9522	3.4259	3.9703	4.5950
17	1.1843	1.4002	1.6528	1.9479	2.2920	2.6928	3.1588	3.7000	4.3276	5.0545
18	1.1961	1.4282	1.7024	2.0258	2.4066	2.8543	3.3799	3.9960	4.7171	5.5599
19	1.2081	1.4568	1.7535	2.1068	2.5270	3.0256	3.6165	4.3157	5.1417	6.1159
20	1.2202	1.4859	1.8061	2.1911	2.6533	3.2071	3.8697	4.6610	5.6044	6.7275
21	1.2324	1.5157	1.8603	2.2788	2.7860	3.3996	4.1406	5.0338	6.1088	7.4002
22	1.2447	1.5460	1.9161	2.3699	2.9253	3.6035	4.4304	5.4365	6.6586	8.1403
23	1.2572	1.5769	1.9736	2.4647	3.0715	3.8197	4.7405	5.8715	7.2579	8.9543
24	1.2697	1.6084	2.0328	2.5633	3.2251	4.0489	5.0724	6.3412	7.9111	9.8497
25	1.2824	1.6406	2.0938	2.6658	3.3864	4.2919	5.4274	6.8485	8.6231	10.834
26	1.2953	1.6734	2.1566	2.7725	3.5557	4.5494	5.8074	7.3964	9.3992	11.918
27	1.3082	1.7069	2.2213	2.8834	3.7335	4.8223	6.2139	7.9881	10.245	13.110
28	1.3213	1.7410	2.2879	2.9987	3.9201	5.1117	6.6488	8.6271	11.167	14.421
29	1.3345	1.7758	2.3566	3.1187	4.1161	5.4184	7.1143	9.3173	12.172	15.863
30	1.3478	1.8114	2.4273	3.2434	4.3219	5.7435	7.6123	10.062	13.267	17.449
40	1.4889	2.2080	3.2620	4.8010	7.0400	10.285	14.974	21.724	31.409	45.259
50	1.6446	2.6916	4.3839	7.1067	11.467	18.420	29.457	46.901	74.357	117.39
60	1.8167	3.2810	5.8916	10.519	18.679	32.987	57.946	101.25	176.03	304.48

Period	12%	14%	15%	16%	18%	20%	24%	28%	32%	36%
1	1.1200	1.1400	1.1500	1.1600	1.1800	1.2000	1.2400	1.2800	1.3200	1.3600
2	1.2544	1.2996	1.3225	1.3456	1.3924	1.4400	1.5376	1.6384	1.7424	1.8496
3	1.4049	1.4815	1.5209	1.5609	1.6430	1.7280	1.9066	2.0972	2.3000	2.5155
4	1.5735	1.6890	1.7490	1.8106	1.9388	2.0736	2.3642	2.6844	3.0360	3.4210
5	1.7623	1.9254	2.0114	2.1003	2.2878	2.4883	2.9316	3.4360	4.0075	4.6526
6	1.9738	2.1950	2.3131	2.4364	2.6996	2.9860	3.6352	4.3980	5.2899	6.3275
7	2.2107	2.5023	2.6600	2.8262	3.1855	3.5832	4.5077	5.6295	6.9826	8.6054
8	2.4760	2.8526	3.0590	3.2784	3.7589	4.2998	5.5895	7.2058	9.2170	11.703
9	2.7731	3.2519	3.5179	3.8030	4.4355	5.1598	6.9310	9.2234	12.166	15.916
10	3.1058	3.7072	4.0456	4.4114	5.2338	6.1917	8.5944	11.805	16.059	21.646
11	3.4785	4.2262	4.6524	5.1173	6.1759	7.4301	10.657	15.111	21.198	29.439
12	3.8960	4.8179	5.3502	5.9360	7.2876	8.9161	13.214	19.342	27.982	40.037
13	4.3635	5.4924	6.1528	6.8858	8.5994	10.699	16.386	24.758	36.937	54.451
14	4.8871	6.2613	7.0757	7.9875	10.147	12.839	20.319	31.691	48.756	74.053
15	5.4736	7.1379	8.1371	9.2655	11.973	15.407	25.195	40.564	64.358	100.71

Appendix A

Period	12%	14%	15%	16%	18%	20%	24%	28%	32%	36%
16	6.1304	8.1372	9.3576	10.748	14.129	18.488	31.242	51.923	84.953	136.96
17	6.8660	9.2765	10.761	12.467	16.672	22.186	38.740	66.461	112.13	186.27
18	7.6900	10.575	12.375	14.462	19.673	26.623	48.038	85.070	148.02	253.33
19	8.6128	12.055	14.231	16.776	23.214	31.948	59.567	108.89	195.39	344.53
20	9.6463	13.743	16.366	19.460	27.393	38.337	73.864	139.37	257.91	468.57
21	10.803	15.667	18.821	22.574	32.323	46.005	91.591	178.40	340.44	637.26
22	12.100	17.861	21.644	26.186	38.142	55.206	113.57	228.35	449.39	866.67
23	13.552	20.361	24.891	30.376	45.007	66.247	140.83	292.30	593.19	1178.6
24	15.178	23.212	28.625	35.236	53.108	79.496	174.63	374.14	783.02	1602.9
25	17.000	26.461	32.918	40.874	62.668	95.396	216.54	478.90	1033.5	2180.0
26	19.040	30.166	37.856	47.414	73.948	114.47	268.51	612.99	1364.3	2964.9
27	21.324	34.389	43.535	55.000	87.259	137.37	332.95	784.63	1800.9	4032.2
28	23.883	39.204	50.065	63.800	102.96	164.84	412.86	1004.3	2377.2	5483.8
29	26.749	44.693	57.575	74.008	121.50	197.81	511.95	1285.5	3137.9	7458.0
30	29.959	50.950	66.211	85.849	143.37	237.37	634.81	1645.5	4142.0	10143.
40	93.050	188.88	267.86	378.72	750.37	1469.7	5455.9	19426.	66520.	*
50	289.00	700.23	1083.6	1670.7	3927.3	9100.4	46890.	*	*	*
60	897.59	2595.9	4383.9	7370.1	20555.	56347.	*	*	*	*

*FVIF > 99,999

218

Appendix B

Compound Sum of An Annuity of $1 Per Period for N Periods

$$FVIFA = \sum_{t=1}^{n} (1 + k)^{t-1}$$

$$FVIFA = \frac{(1 + k)^n - 1}{k}$$

Number of Periods	1%	2%	3%	4%	5%	6%	7%	8%	9%	10%
1	1.0000	1.0000	1.0000	1.0000	1.0000	1.0000	1.0000	1.0000	1.0000	1.0000
2	2.0100	2.0200	2.0300	2.0400	2.0500	2.0600	2.0700	2.0800	2.0900	2.1000
3	3.0301	3.0604	3.0909	3.1216	3.1525	3.1836	3.2149	3.2464	3.2781	3.3100
4	4.0604	4.1216	4.1836	4.2465	4.3101	4.3746	4.4399	4.5061	4.5731	4.6410
5	5.1010	5.2040	5.3091	5.4163	5.5256	5.6371	5.7507	5.8666	5.9847	6.1051
6	6.1520	6.3081	6.4684	6.6330	6.8019	6.9753	7.1533	7.3359	7.5233	7.7156
7	7.2135	7.4343	7.6625	7.8983	8.1420	8.3938	8.6540	8.9228	9.2004	9.4872
8	8.2857	8.5830	8.8923	9.2142	9.5491	9.8975	10.259	10.636	11.028	11.435
9	9.3685	9.7546	10.159	10.582	11.026	11.491	11.978	12.487	13.021	13.579
10	10.462	10.949	11.463	12.006	12.577	13.180	13.816	14.486	15.192	15.937
11	11.566	12.168	12.807	13.486	14.206	14.971	15.783	16.645	17.560	18.531
12	12.682	13.412	14.192	15.025	15.917	16.869	17.888	18.977	20.140	21.384
13	13.809	14.680	15.617	16.626	17.713	18.882	20.140	21.495	22.953	24.522
14	14.947	15.973	17.086	18.291	19.598	21.015	22.550	24.214	26.019	27.975
15	16.096	17.293	18.598	20.023	21.578	23.276	25.129	27.152	29.360	31.772

Appendix B

Number of Periods	1%	2%	3%	4%	5%	6%	7%	8%	9%	10%
16	17.257	18.639	20.156	21.824	23.657	25.672	27.888	30.324	33.003	35.949
17	18.430	20.012	21.761	23.697	25.840	28.212	30.840	33.750	36.973	40.544
18	19.614	21.412	23.414	25.645	28.132	30.905	33.999	37.450	41.301	45.599
19	20.810	22.840	25.116	27.671	30.539	33.760	37.379	41.446	46.018	51.159
20	22.019	24.297	26.870	29.778	33.066	36.785	40.995	45.762	51.160	57.275
21	23.239	25.783	28.676	31.969	35.719	39.992	44.865	50.422	56.764	64.002
22	24.471	27.299	30.536	34.248	38.505	43.392	49.005	55.456	62.873	71.402
23	25.716	28.845	32.452	36.617	41.430	46.995	53.436	60.893	69.531	79.543
24	26.973	30.421	34.426	39.082	44.502	50.815	58.176	66.764	76.789	88.497
25	28.243	32.030	36.459	41.645	47.727	54.864	63.249	73.105	84.700	98.347
26	29.525	33.670	38.553	44.311	51.113	59.156	68.676	79.954	93.323	109.18
27	30.820	35.344	40.709	47.084	54.669	63.705	74.483	87.350	102.72	121.09
28	32.129	37.051	42.930	49.967	58.402	68.528	80.697	95.338	112.96	134.20
29	33.450	38.792	45.218	52.966	62.322	73.639	87.346	103.96	124.13	148.63
30	34.784	40.568	47.575	56.084	66.438	79.058	94.460	113.28	136.30	164.49
40	48.886	60.402	75.401	95.025	120.79	154.76	199.63	259.05	337.88	442.59
50	64.463	84.579	112.79	152.66	209.34	290.33	406.52	573.76	815.08	1163.9
60	81.669	114.05	163.05	237.99	353.58	533.12	813.52	1253.2	1944.7	3034.8

Number of Periods	12%	14%	15%	16%	18%	20%	24%	28%	32%	36%
1	1.0000	1.0000	1.0000	1.0000	1.0000	1.0000	1.0000	1.0000	1.0000	1.0000
2	2.1200	2.1400	2.1500	2.1600	2.1800	2.2000	2.2400	2.2800	2.3200	2.3600
3	3.3744	3.4396	3.4725	3.5056	3.5724	3.6400	3.7776	3.9184	4.0624	4.2096
4	4.7793	4.9211	4.9934	5.0665	5.2154	5.3680	5.6842	6.0156	6.3624	6.7251
5	6.3528	6.6101	6.7424	6.8771	7.1542	7.4416	8.0484	8.6999	9.3983	10.146
6	8.1152	8.5355	8.7537	8.9775	9.4420	9.9299	10.980	12.135	13.405	14.798
7	10.089	10.730	11.066	11.413	12.141	12.915	14.615	16.533	18.695	21.126
8	12.299	13.232	13.726	14.240	15.327	16.499	19.122	22.163	25.678	29.731
9	14.775	16.085	16.785	17.518	19.085	20.798	24.712	29.369	34.895	41.435
10	17.548	19.337	20.303	21.321	23.521	25.958	31.643	38.592	47.061	57.351
11	20.654	23.044	24.349	25.732	28.755	32.150	40.237	50.398	63.121	78.998
12	24.133	27.270	29.001	30.850	34.931	39.580	50.894	65.510	84.320	108.43
13	28.029	32.088	34.351	36.786	42.218	48.496	64.109	84.852	112.30	148.47
14	32.392	37.581	40.504	43.672	50.818	59.195	80.496	109.61	149.23	202.92
15	37.279	43.842	47.580	51.659	60.965	72.035	100.81	141.30	197.99	276.97

Appendix B

Number of Periods	12%	14%	15%	16%	18%	20%	24%	28%	32%	36%
16	42.753	50.980	55.717	60.925	72.939	87.442	126.01	181.86	262.35	377.69
17	48.883	59.117	65.075	71.673	87.068	105.93	157.25	233.79	347.30	514.66
18	55.749	68.394	75.836	84.140	103.74	128.11	195.99	300.25	459.44	700.93
19	63.439	78.969	88.211	98.603	123.41	154.74	244.03	385.32	607.47	954.27
20	72.052	91.024	102.44	115.37	146.62	186.68	303.60	494.21	802.86	1298.8
21	81.698	104.76	118.81	134.84	174.02	225.02	377.46	633.59	1060.7	1767.3
22	92.502	120.43	137.63	157.41	206.34	271.03	469.05	811.99	1401.2	2404.6
23	104.60	138.29	159.27	183.60	244.48	326.23	582.62	1040.3	1850.6	3271.3
24	118.15	158.65	184.16	213.97	289.49	392.48	723.46	1332.6	2443.8	4449.9
25	133.33	181.87	212.79	249.21	342.60	471.98	898.09	1706.8	3226.8	6052.9
26	150.33	208.33	245.71	290.08	405.27	567.37	1114.6	2185.7	4260.4	8233.0
27	169.37	238.49	283.56	337.50	479.22	681.85	1383.1	2798.7	5624.7	11197.9
28	190.69	272.88	327.10	392.50	566.48	819.22	1716.0	3583.3	7425.6	15230.2
29	214.58	312.09	377.16	456.30	669.44	964.06	2128.9	4587.6	9802.9	20714.1
30	241.33	356.78	434.74	530.31	790.94	1181.8	2640.9	5873.2	12940.	28172.2
40	767.09	1342.0	1779.0	2360.7	4163.2	7343.8	22728.	69377.	*	*
50	2400.0	4994.5	7217.7	10435.	21813.	45497.	*	*	*	*
60	7471.6	18535.	29219.	46057.	*	*	*	*	*	*

*FVIFA > 99,999

Appendix C

Present Value of $1

Period	1%	2%	3%	4%	5%	6%	7%	8%	9%	10%
1	.9901	.9804	.9709	.9615	.9524	.9434	.9346	.9259	.9174	.9091
2	.9803	.9612	.9426	.9246	.9070	.8900	.8734	.8573	.8417	.8264
3	.9706	.9423	.9151	.8890	.8638	.8396	.8163	.7938	.7722	.7513
4	.9610	.9238	.8885	.8548	.8227	.7921	.7629	.7350	.7084	.6830
5	.9515	.9057	.8626	.8219	.7835	.7473	.7130	.6806	.6499	.6209
6	.9420	.8880	.8375	.7903	.7462	.7050	.6663	.6302	.5963	.5645
7	.9327	.8706	.8131	.7599	.7107	.6651	.6227	.5835	.5470	.5132
8	.9235	.8535	.7894	.7307	.6768	.6274	.5820	.5403	.5019	.4665
9	.9143	.8368	.7664	.7026	.6446	.5919	.5439	.5002	.4604	.4241
10	.9053	.8203	.7441	.6756	.6139	.5584	.5083	.4632	.4224	.3855
11	.8963	.8043	.7224	.6496	.5847	.5268	.4751	.4289	.3875	.3505
12	.8874	.7885	.7014	.6246	.5568	.4970	.4440	.3971	.3555	.3186
13	.8787	.7730	.6810	.6006	.5303	.4688	.4150	.3677	.3262	.2897
14	.8700	.7579	.6611	.5775	.5051	.4423	.3878	.3405	.2992	.2633
15	.8613	.7430	.6419	.5553	.4810	.4173	.3624	.3152	.2745	.2394

Appendix C

Period	1%	2%	3%	4%	5%	6%	7%	8%	9%	10%
16	.8528	.7284	.6232	.5339	.4581	.3936	.3387	.2919	.2519	.2176
17	.8444	.7142	.6050	.5134	.4363	.3714	.3166	.2703	.2311	.1978
18	.8360	.7002	.5874	.4936	.4155	.3503	.2959	.2502	.2120	.1799
19	.8277	.6864	.5703	.4746	.3957	.3305	.2765	.2317	.1945	.1635
20	.8195	.6730	.5537	.4564	.3769	.3118	.2584	.2145	.1784	.1486
21	.8114	.6598	.5375	.4388	.3589	.2942	.2415	.1987	.1637	.1351
22	.8034	.6468	.5219	.4220	.3418	.2775	.2257	.1839	.1502	.1228
23	.7954	.6342	.5067	.4057	.3256	.2618	.2109	.1703	.1378	.1117
24	.7876	.6217	.4919	.3901	.3101	.2470	.1971	.1577	.1264	.1015
25	.7798	.6095	.4776	.3751	.2953	.2330	.1842	.1460	.1160	.0923
26	.7720	.5976	.4637	.3607	.2812	.2198	.1722	.1352	.1064	.0839
27	.7644	.5859	.4502	.3468	.2678	.2074	.1609	.1252	.0976	.0763
28	.7568	.5744	.4371	.3335	.2551	.1956	.1504	.1159	.0895	.0693
29	.7493	.5631	.4243	.3207	.2429	.1846	.1406	.1073	.0822	.0630
30	.7419	.5521	.4120	.3083	.2314	.1741	.1314	.0994	.0754	.0573
35	.7059	.5000	.3554	.2534	.1813	.1301	.0937	.0676	.0490	.0356
40	.6717	.4529	.3066	.2083	.1420	.0972	.0668	.0460	.0318	.0221
45	.6391	.4102	.2644	.1712	.1113	.0727	.0476	.0313	.0207	.0137
50	.6080	.3715	.2281	.1407	.0872	.0543	.0339	.0213	.0134	.0085
55	.5785	.3365	.1968	.1157	.0683	.0406	.0242	.0145	.0087	.0053

Period	12%	14%	15%	16%	18%	20%	24%	28%	32%	36%
1	.8929	.8772	.8696	.8621	.8475	.8333	.8065	.7813	.7576	.7353
2	.7972	.7695	.7561	.7432	.7182	.6944	.6504	.6104	.5739	.5407
3	.7118	.6750	.6575	.6407	.6086	.5787	.5245	.4768	.4348	.3975
4	.6355	.5921	.5718	.5523	.5158	.4823	.4230	.3725	.3294	.2923
5	.5674	.5194	.4972	.4761	.4371	.4019	.3411	.2910	.2495	.2149
6	.5066	.4556	.4323	.4104	.3704	.3349	.2751	.2274	.1890	.1580
7	.4523	.3996	.3759	.3538	.3139	.2791	.2218	.1776	.1432	.1162
8	.4039	.3506	.3269	.3050	.2660	.2326	.1789	.1388	.1085	.0854
9	.3606	.3075	.2843	.2630	.2255	.1938	.1443	.1084	.0822	.0628
10	.3220	.2697	.2472	.2267	.1911	.1615	.1164	.0847	.0623	.0462
11	.2875	.2366	.2149	.1954	.1619	.1346	.0938	.0662	.0472	.0340
12	.2567	.2076	.1869	.1685	.1372	.1122	.0757	.0517	.0357	.0250
13	.2292	.1821	.1625	.1452	.1163	.0935	.0610	.0404	.0271	.0184
14	.2046	.1597	.1413	.1252	.0985	.0779	.0492	.0316	.0205	.0135
15	.1827	.1401	.1229	.1079	.0835	.0649	.0397	.0247	.0155	.0099

Period	12%	14%	15%	16%	18%	20%	24%	28%	32%	36%
16	.1631	.1229	.1069	.0930	.0708	.0541	.0320	.0193	.0118	.0073
17	.1456	.1078	.0929	.0802	.0600	.0451	.0258	.0150	.0089	.0054
18	.1300	.0946	.0808	.0691	.0508	.0376	.0208	.0118	.0068	.0039
19	.1161	.0829	.0703	.0596	.0431	.0313	.0168	.0092	.0051	.0029
20	.1037	.0728	.0611	.0514	.0365	.0261	.0135	.0072	.0039	.0021
21	.0926	.0638	.0531	.0443	.0309	.0217	.0109	.0056	.0029	.0016
22	.0826	.0560	.0462	.0382	.0262	.0181	.0088	.0044	.0022	.0012
23	.0738	.0491	.0402	.0329	.0222	.0151	.0071	.0034	.0017	.0008
24	.0659	.0431	.0349	.0284	.0188	.0126	.0057	.0027	.0013	.0006
25	.0588	.0378	.0304	.0245	.0160	.0105	.0046	.0021	.0010	.0005
26	.0525	.0331	.0264	.0211	.0135	.0087	.0037	.0016	.0007	.0003
27	.0469	.0291	.0230	.0182	.0115	.0073	.0030	.0013	.0006	.0002
28	.0419	.0255	.0200	.0157	.0097	.0061	.0024	.0010	.0004	.0002
29	.0374	.0224	.0174	.0135	.0082	.0051	.0020	.0008	.0003	.0001
30	.0334	.0196	.0151	.0116	.0070	.0042	.0016	.0006	.0002	.0001
35	.0189	.0102	.0075	.0055	.0030	.0017	.0005	.0002	.0001	*
40	.0107	.0053	.0037	.0026	.0013	.0007	.0002	.0001	*	*
45	.0061	.0027	.0019	.0013	.0006	.0003	.0001	*	*	*
50	.0035	.0014	.0009	.0006	.0003	.0001	*	*	*	*
55	.0020	.0007	.0005	.0003	.0001	*	*	*	*	*

*The factor is zero to four decimal places

Appendix D

Present Value of an Annuity of $1 Per Period for N Periods

$$PVIFA = \sum_{i=1}^{n} \frac{1}{(1+k)^i} = \frac{1 - \dfrac{1}{(1+k)^n}}{k}$$

Number of Payments	1%	2%	3%	4%	5%	6%	7%	8%	9%
1	0.9901	0.9804	0.9709	0.9615	0.9524	0.9434	0.9346	0.9259	0.9174
2	1.9704	1.9416	1.9135	1.8861	1.8594	1.8334	1.8080	1.7833	1.7591
3	2.9410	2.8839	2.8286	2.7751	2.7232	2.6730	2.6243	2.5771	2.5313
4	3.9020	3.8077	3.7171	3.6299	3.5460	3.4651	3.3872	3.3121	3.2397
5	4.8534	4.7135	4.5797	4.4518	4.3295	4.2124	4.1002	3.9927	3.8897
6	5.7955	5.6014	5.4172	5.2421	5.0757	4.9173	4.7665	4.6229	4.4859
7	6.7282	6.4720	6.2303	6.0021	5.7864	5.5824	5.3893	5.2064	5.0330
8	7.6517	7.3255	7.0197	6.7327	6.4632	6.2098	5.9713	5.7466	5.5348
9	8.5660	8.1622	7.7861	7.4353	7.1078	6.8017	6.5152	6.2469	5.9952
10	9.4713	8.9826	8.5302	8.1109	7.7217	7.3601	7.0236	6.7101	6.4177
11	10.3676	9.7868	9.2526	8.7605	8.3064	7.8869	7.4987	7.1390	6.8052
12	11.2551	10.5753	9.9540	9.3851	8.8633	8.3838	7.9427	7.5361	7.1607
13	12.1337	11.3484	10.6350	9.9856	9.3936	8.8527	8.3577	7.9038	7.4869
14	13.0037	12.1062	11.2961	10.5631	9.8986	9.2950	8.7455	8.2442	7.7862
15	13.8651	12.8493	11.9379	11.1184	10.3797	9.7122	9.1079	8.5595	8.0607

Appendix D

Number of Payments	1%	2%	3%	4%	5%	6%	7%	8%	9%
16	14.7179	13.5777	12.5611	11.6523	10.8378	10.1059	9.4466	8.8514	8.3126
17	15.5623	14.2919	13.1661	12.1657	11.2741	10.4773	9.7632	9.1216	8.5436
18	16.3983	14.9920	13.7535	12.6593	11.6896	10.8276	10.0591	9.3719	8.7556
19	17.2260	15.6785	14.3238	13.1339	12.0853	11.1581	10.3356	9.6036	8.9501
20	18.0456	16.3514	14.8775	13.5903	12.4622	11.4699	10.5940	9.8181	9.1285
21	18.8570	17.0112	15.4150	14.0292	12.8212	11.7641	10.8355	10.0168	9.2922
22	19.6604	17.6580	15.9369	14.4511	13.1630	12.0416	11.0612	10.2007	9.4424
23	20.4558	18.2922	16.4436	14.8568	13.4886	12.3034	11.2722	10.3711	9.5802
24	21.2434	18.9139	16.9355	15.2470	13.7986	12.5504	11.4693	10.5288	9.7066
25	22.0232	19.5235	17.4131	15.6221	14.0939	12.7834	11.6536	10.6748	9.8226
26	22.7952	20.1210	17.8768	15.9828	14.3752	13.0032	11.8258	10.8100	9.9290
27	23.5596	20.7069	18.3270	16.3296	14.6430	13.2105	11.9867	10.9352	10.0266
28	24.3164	21.2813	18.7641	16.6631	14.8981	13.4062	12.1371	11.0511	10.1161
29	25.0658	21.8444	19.1885	16.9837	15.1411	13.5907	12.2777	11.1584	10.1983
30	25.8077	22.3965	19.6004	17.2920	15.3725	13.7648	12.4090	11.2578	10.2737
35	29.4086	24.9986	21.4872	18.6646	16.3742	14.4982	12.9477	11.6546	10.5668
40	32.8347	27.3555	23.1148	19.7928	17.1591	15.0463	13.3317	11.9246	10.7574
45	36.0945	29.4902	24.5187	20.7200	17.7741	15.4558	13.6055	12.1084	10.8812
50	39.1961	31.4236	25.7298	21.4822	18.2559	15.7619	13.8007	12.2335	10.9617
55	42.1472	33.1748	26.7744	22.1086	18.6335	15.9905	13.9399	12.3186	11.0140

Number of Payments	10%	12%	14%	15%	16%	18%	20%	24%	28%	32%
1	0.9091	0.8929	0.8772	0.8696	0.8621	0.8475	0.8333	0.8065	0.7813	0.7576
2	1.7355	1.6901	1.6467	1.6257	1.6052	1.5656	1.5278	1.4568	1.3916	1.3315
3	2.4869	2.4018	2.3216	2.2832	2.2459	2.1743	2.1065	1.9813	1.8684	1.7663
4	3.1699	3.0373	2.9137	2.8550	2.7982	2.6901	2.5887	2.4043	2.2410	2.0957
5	3.7908	3.6048	3.4331	3.3522	3.2743	3.1272	2.9906	2.7454	2.5320	2.3452
6	4.3553	4.1114	3.8887	3.7845	3.6847	3.4976	3.3255	3.0205	2.7594	2.5342
7	4.8684	4.5638	4.2883	4.1604	4.0386	3.8115	3.6046	3.2423	2.9370	2.6775
8	5.3349	4.9676	4.6389	4.4873	4.3436	4.0776	3.8372	3.4212	3.0758	2.7860
9	5.7590	5.3282	4.9464	4.7716	4.6065	4.3030	4.0310	3.5655	3.1842	2.8681
10	6.1446	5.6502	5.2161	5.0188	4.8332	4.4941	4.1925	3.6819	3.2689	2.9304
11	6.4951	5.9377	5.4527	5.2337	5.0286	4.6560	4.3271	3.7757	3.3351	2.9776
12	6.8137	6.1944	5.6603	5.4206	5.1971	4.7932	4.4392	3.8514	3.3868	3.0133
13	7.1034	6.4235	5.8424	5.5831	5.3423	4.9095	4.5327	3.9124	3.4272	3.0404
14	7.3667	6.6282	6.0021	5.7245	5.4675	5.0081	4.6106	3.9616	3.4587	3.0609
15	7.6061	6.8109	6.1422	5.8474	5.5755	5.0916	4.6755	4.0013	3.4834	3.0764

Appendix D

Number of Payments	10%	12%	14%	15%	16%	18%	20%	24%	28%	32%
16	7.8237	6.9740	6.2651	5.9542	5.6685	5.1624	4.7296	4.0333	3.5026	3.0882
17	8.0216	7.1196	6.3729	6.0472	5.7487	5.2223	4.7746	4.0591	3.5177	3.0971
18	8.2014	7.2497	6.4674	6.1280	5.8178	5.2732	4.8122	4.0799	3.5294	3.1039
19	8.3649	7.3658	6.5504	6.1982	5.8775	5.3162	4.8435	4.0967	3.5386	3.1090
20	8.5136	7.4694	6.6231	6.2593	5.9288	5.3527	4.8696	4.1103	3.5458	3.1129
21	8.6487	7.5620	6.6870	6.3125	5.9731	5.3837	4.8913	4.1212	3.5514	3.1158
22	8.7715	7.6446	6.7429	6.3587	6.0113	5.4099	4.9094	4.1300	3.5558	3.1180
23	8.8832	7.7184	6.7921	6.3988	6.0442	5.4321	4.9245	4.1371	3.5592	3.1197
24	8.9847	7.7843	6.8351	6.4338	6.0726	5.4510	4.9371	4.1428	3.5619	3.1210
25	9.0770	7.8431	6.8729	6.4642	6.0971	5.4669	4.9476	4.1474	3.5640	3.1220
26	9.1609	7.8957	6.9061	6.4906	6.1182	5.4804	4.9563	4.1511	3.5656	3.1227
27	9.2372	7.9426	6.9352	6.5135	6.1364	5.4919	4.9636	4.1542	3.5669	3.1233
28	9.3066	7.9844	6.9607	6.5335	6.1520	5.5016	4.9697	4.1566	3.5679	3.1237
29	9.3696	8.0218	6.9830	6.5509	6.1656	5.5098	4.9747	4.1585	3.5687	3.1240
30	9.4269	8.0552	7.0027	6.5660	6.1772	5.5168	4.9789	4.1601	3.5693	3.1242
35	9.6442	8.1755	7.0700	6.6166	6.2153	5.5386	4.9915	4.1644	3.5708	3.1248
40	9.7791	8.2438	7.1050	6.6418	6.2335	5.5482	4.9966	4.1659	3.5712	3.1250
45	9.8628	8.2825	7.1232	6.6543	6.2421	5.5523	4.9986	4.1664	3.5714	3.1250
50	9.9148	8.3045	7.1327	6.6605	6.2463	5.5541	4.9995	4.1666	3.5714	3.1250
55	9.9471	8.3170	7.1376	6.6636	6.2482	5.5549	4.9998	4.1666	3.5714	3.1250

Appendix E

Uniform Limited Partnership Act

Be it enacted, etc., as follows:

Sec. 1. (Limited Partnership Defined.) A limited partnership is a partnership formed by two or more persons under the provisions of Section 2, having as members one or more general partners and one or more limited partners. The limited partners as such shall not be bound by the obligations of the partnership.

Sec. 2. (Formation.) (1) Two or more persons desiring to form a limited partnership shall

(a) Sign and swear to a certificate, which shall state

    I. The name of the partnership,
    II. The character of the business,
    III. The location of the principal place of business,
    IV. The name and place of residence of each member; general and limited partners being respectively designated,
    V. The term for which the partnership is to exist,
    VI. The amount of cash and a description of and the agreed value of the other property contributed by each limited partner,
    VII. The additional contributions, if any, agreed to be made by each limited partner and the times at which or events on the happening of which they shall be made,
    VIII. The time, if agreed upon, when the contribution of each limited partner is to be returned,
    IX. The share of the profits or the other compensation by way of income which each limited partner shall receive by reason of his contribution,
    X. The right, if given, of a limited partner to substitute an assignee as contributor in his place, and the terms and conditions of the substitution,
    XI. The right, if given, of the partners to admit additional limited partners,
    XII. The right, if given, of one or more of the limited partners to priority over other limited partners, as to contributions or as to compensation by way of income, and the nature of such priority,
    XIII. The right, if given, of the remaining general partner or partners to continue the business on the death, retirement or insanity of a general partner, and
    XIV. The right, if given, of a limited partner to demand and receive property other than cash in return for his contribution.

(b) File for record the certificate in the office of [here designate the proper office].

(2) A limited partnership is formed if there has been substantial compliance in good faith with the requirements of paragraph (1).

Sec. 3. (Business Which may Be Carried On.) A limited partnership may carry on any business which a partnership without limited partners may carry on, except [here designate the business to be prohibited].

Sec. 4. (Character of Limited Partner's Contribution.) The contributions of a limited partner may be cash or other property, but not services.

Sec. 5. (A Name Not to Contain Surname of Limited Partner; Exceptions.) (1) The surname of a limited partner shall not appear in the partnership name, unless

(a) It is also the surname of a general partner, or

(b) Prior to the time when the limited partner became such the business had been carried on under a name in which his surname appeared.

(2) A limited partner whose name appears in a partnership name contrary to the provisions of paragraph (1) is liable as a general partner to partnership creditors who extend credit to the partnership without actual knowledge that he is not a general partner.

Sec. 6. (Liability for False Statements in Certificate.) If the certificate contains a false statement, one who suffers loss by reliance on such statement may hold liable any party to the certificate who knew the statement to be false.

(a) At the time he signed the certificate, or

(b) Subsequently, but within a sufficient time before the statement was relied upon to enable him to cancel or amend the certificate, or to file a petition for its cancellation or amendment as provided in Section 25(3).

Sec. 7. (Limited Partner Not Liable to Creditors.) A limited partner shall not become liable as a general partner unless, in addition to the exercise of his rights and powers as a limited partner, he takes part in the control of the business.

Sec. 8. (Admission of Additional Limited Partners.) After the formation of a limited partnership, additional limited partners may be admitted upon filing an amendment to the original certificate in accordance with the requirements of Section 25.

Sec. 9. (Rights, Powers and Liabilities of a General Partner.) (1) A general partner shall have all the rights and powers and be subject to all the restrictions and liabilities of a partner in a partnership without limited part-

*National Conference of Commissioners on Uniform State Laws (1976).

Appendix E

ners, except that without the written consent or ratification of the specific act by all the limited partners, a general partner or all of the general partners have no authority to

(a) Do any act in contravention of the certificate,

(b) Do any act which would make it impossible to carry on the ordinary business of the partnership,

(c) Confess a judgment against the partnership,

(d) Possess partnership property, or assign their rights in specific partnership property, for other than a partnership purpose,

(e) Admit a person as a general partner,

(f) Admit a person as a limited partner, unless the right to do so is given in the certificate,

(g) Continue the business with partnership property on the death, retirement or insanity of a general partner, unless the right so to do is given in the certificate.

Sec. 10. (Rights of a Limited Partner.) (1) A limited partner shall have the same rights as a general partner to

(a) Have the partnership books kept at the principal place of business of the partnership, and at all times to inspect and copy any of them,

(b) Have on demand true and full information of all things affecting the partnership, and a formal account of partnership affairs, whenever circumstances render it just and reasonable, and

(c) Have dissolution and winding up by decree of court.

(2) A limited partner shall have the right to receive a share of the profits or other compensation by way of income, and to the return of his contribution as provided in Sections 15 and 16.

Sec. 11. (Status of Person Erroneously Believing Himself a Limited Partner.) A person who has contributed to the capital of a business conducted by a person or partnership erroneously believing that he has become a limited partner in a limited partnership, is not, by reason of his exercise of the rights of a limited partner, a general partner with the person or in the partnership carrying on the business, or bound by the obligations of such person or partnership; provided that on ascertaining the mistake he promptly renounces his interest in the profits of the business, or other compensation by way of income.

Sec. 12. (One Person Both General and Limited Partner.) (1) A person may be a general partner and a limited partner in the same partnership at the same time.

(2) A person who is a general, and also at the same time a limited partner, shall have all the rights and powers and be subject to all the restrictions of a general partner; except that,

in respect to his contribution, he shall have the rights against the other members which he would have had if he were not also a general partner.

Sec. 13. (Loans and Other Business Transactions with Limited Partner.) (1) A limited partner also may loan money to and transact other business with the partnership, and, unless he is also a general partner, receive on account of resulting claims against the partnership, with general creditors, a pro rata share of the assets. No limited partner shall in respect to any such claim

(a) Receive or hold as collateral security any partnership property, or

(b) Receive from a general partner or the partnership any payment, conveyance, or release from liability, if at the time the assets of the partnership are not sufficient to discharge partnership liabilities to persons not claiming as general or limited partners.

(2) The receiving of collateral security, or a payment, conveyance, or release in violation of the provisions of paragraph (1) is a fraud on the creditors of the partnership.

Sec. 14. (Relation of Limited Partners Inter Se.) Where there are several limited partners the members may agree that one or more of the limited partners shall have a priority over other limited partners as to the return of their contributions, as to their compensation by way of income, or as to any other matter. If such an agreement is made it shall be stated in the certificate, and in the absence of such a statement all the limited partners shall stand upon equal footing.

Sec. 15. (Compensation of Limited Partner.) A limited partner may receive from the partnership the share of the profits or the compensation by way of income stipulated for in the certificate; provided, that after such payment is made, whether from the property of the partnership or that of a general partner, the partnership assets are in excess of all liabilities of the partnership except liabilities to limited partners on account of their contributions and to general partners.

Sec. 16. (Withdrawal or Reduction of Limited Partner's Contribution.) (1) A limited partner shall not receive from a general partner or out of partnership property any part of his contribution until

(a) All liabilities of the partnership, except liabilities to general partners and to limited partners on account of their contributions, have been paid or there remains property of the partnership sufficient to pay them,

(b) The consent of all members is had, unless the return of the contribution may be right-

248

fully demanded under the provisions of paragraph (2), and

(c) The certificate is cancelled or so amended as to set forth the withdrawal or reduction.

(2) Subject to the provisions of paragraph (1) a limited partner may rightfully demand the return of his contribution

(a) On the dissolution of a partnership, or

(b) When the date specified in the certificate for its return has arrived, or

(c) After he has given six months' notice in writing to all other members, if no time is specified in the certificate either for the return of the contribution or for the dissolution of the partnership,

(3) In the absence of any statement in the certificate to the contrary or the consent of all members, a limited partner, irrespective of the nature of his contribution, has only the right to demand and receive cash in return for his contribution.

(4) A limited partner may have the partnership dissolved and its affairs wound up when

(a) He rightfully but unsuccessfully demands the return of his contribution, or

(b) The other liabilities of the partnership have not been paid, or the partnership property is insufficient for their payment as required by paragraph (1a) and the limited partner would otherwise be entitled to the return of his contribution.

Sec. 17. (Liability of Limited Partner to Partnership.)

(1) A limited partner is liable to the partnership

(a) For the difference between his contribution as actually made and that stated in the certificate as having been made, and

(b) For any unpaid contribution which he agreed in the certificate to make in the future at the time and on the conditions stated in the certificate.

(2) A limited partner holds as trustee for the partnership

(a) Specific property stated in the certificate as contributed by him, but which was not contributed or which has been wrongfully returned, and

(b) Money or other property wrongfully paid or conveyed to him on account of his contribution.

(3) The liabilities of a limited partner as set forth in this section can be waived or compromised only by the consent of all members; but a waiver or compromise shall not affect the right of a creditor of a partnership, who extended credit or whose claim arose after the filing and before a cancellation or amendment of the certificate, to enforce such liabilities.

(4) When a contributor has rightfully received the return in whole or in part of the capital of his contribution, he is nevertheless liable to the partnership for any sum, not in excess of such return with interest, necessary to discharge its liabilities to all creditors who extended credit or whose claims arose before such return.

Sec. 18. (Nature of Limited Partner's Interest in Partnership.)

A limited partner's interest in the partnership is personal property.

Sec. 19. (Assignment of Limited Partner's Interest.)

(1) A limited partner's interest is assignable.

(2) A substituted limited partner is a person admitted to all the rights of a limited partner who has died or has assigned his interest in a partnership.

(3) An assignee, who does not become a substituted limited partner, has no right to require any information or account of the partnership transactions or to inspect the partnership books; he is only entitled to receive the share of the profits or other compensation by way of income, or the return of his contribution, to which his assignor would otherwise be entitled.

(4) An assignee shall have the right to become a substituted limited partner if all the members (except the assignor) consent thereto or if the assignor, being thereunto empowered by the certificate, gives the assignee that right.

(5) An assignee becomes a substituted limited partner when the certificate is appropriately amended in accordance with Section 25.

(6) The substituted limited partner has all the rights and powers, and is subject to all the restrictions and liabilities of his assignor, except those liabilities of which he was ignorant at the time he became a limited partner and which could not be ascertained from the certificate.

(7) The substitution of the assignee as a limited partner does not release the assignor from liability to the partnership under Sections 6 and 17

Sec. 20. (Effect of Retirement, Death or Insanity of a Genera. Partner.)

The retirement, death or insanity of a general partner dissolves the partnership, unless the business is continued by the remaining general partners

(a) Under a right so to do stated in the certificate, or

(b) With the consent of all members.

Sec. 21. (Death of Limited Partner.)

(1) On the death of a limited partner his executor or administrator shall have all the rights of a limited partner for the purpose of settling his estate, and such power as the deceased had to constitute his assignee a substituted limited partner.

(2) The estate of a deceased limited partner

shall be liable for all his liabilities as a limited partner.

Sec. 22. (Rights of Creditors of Limited Partner.) (1) On due application to a court of competent jurisdiction by any judgment creditor of a limited partner, the court may charge the interest of the indebted limited partner with payment of the unsatisfied amount of the judgment debt; and may appoint a receiver, and make all other orders, directions, and inquiries which the circumstances of the case may require.

In those states where a creditor on beginning an action can attach debts due the defendant before he has obtained a judgment against the defendant it is recommended that paragraph (1) of this section read as follows:

On due application to a court of competent jurisdiction by any creditor of a limited partner, the court may charge the interest of the indebted limited partner with payment of the unsatisfied amount of such claim; and may appoint a receiver, and make all other orders, directions, and inquiries which the circumstances of the case may require.

(2) The interest may be redeemed with the separate property of any general partner, but may not be redeemed with partnership property.

(3) The remedies conferred by paragraph (1) shall not be deemed exclusive of others which may exist.

(4) Nothing in this act shall be held to deprive a limited partner of his statutory exemption.

Sec. 23. (Distribution of Assets.) (1) In settling accounts after dissolution the liabilities of the partnership shall be entitled to payment in the following order:

(a) Those to creditors, in the order of priority as provided by law, except those to limited partners on account of their contributions, and to general partners,

(b) Those to limited partners in respect to their share of the profits and other compensation by way of income on their contributions,

(c) Those to limited partners in respect to the capital of their contributions,

(d) Those to general partners other than for capital and profits,

(e) Those to general partners in respect to profits,

(f) Those to general partners in respect to capital.

(2) Subject to any statement in the certificate or to subsequent agreement, limited partners share in the partnership assets in respect to their claims for capital, and in respect to their claims for profits or for compensation by way of income on their contributions respectively, in proportion to the respective amounts of such claims.

Sec. 24. (When Certificate Shall Be Cancelled or Amended.) (1) The certificate shall be cancelled when the partnership is dissolved or all limited partners cease to be such.

(2) A certificate shall be amended when

(a) There is a change in the name of the partnership or in the amount or character of the contribution of any limited partner,

(b) A person is substituted as a limited partner,

(c) An additional limited partner is admitted,

(d) A person is admitted as a general partner,

(e) A general partner retires, dies or becomes insane, and the business is continued under Section 20,

(f) There is a change in the character of the business of the partnership,

(g) There is a false or erroneous statement in the certificate,

(h) There is a change in the time as stated in the certificate for the dissolution of the partnership or for the return of a contribution,

(i) A time is fixed for the dissolution of the partnership, or the return of a contribution, no time having been specified in the certificate, or

(j) The members desire to make a change in any other statement in the certificate in order that it shall accurately represent the agreement between them.

Sec. 25. (Requirements for Amendment and for Cancellation of Certificate.) (1) The writing to amend a certificate shall

(a) Conform to the requirements of Section 2(1a) as far as necessary to set forth clearly the change in the certificate which it is desired to make, and

(b) Be signed and sworn to by all members, and an amendment substituting a limited partner or adding a limited or general partner shall be signed also by the member to be substituted or added, and when a limited partner is to be substituted, the amendment shall also be signed by the assigning limited partner.

(2) The writing to cancel a certificate shall be signed by all members.

(3) A person desiring the cancellation or amendment of a certificate, if any person designated in paragraphs (1) and (2) as a person who must execute the writing refuses to do so, may petition the [here designate the proper court] to direct a cancellation or amendment thereof.

(4) If the court finds that the petitioner has a right to have the writing executed by a person who refuses to do so, it shall order the [here designate the responsible official in the office designated in Section 2] in the office where the certificate is recorded to record the cancellation or amendment of the certificate; and where the

certificate is to be amended, the court also cause to be filed for record in said office a certified copy of its decree setting forth the amendment.

(5) A certificate is amended or cancelled when there is filed for record in the office [here designate the office designated in Section 2] where the certificate is recorded

(a) A writing in accordance with the provisions of paragraph (1), or (2) or

(b) A certified copy of the order of court in accordance with the provisions of paragraph (4).

(6) After the certificate is duly amended in accordance with this section, the amended certificate shall thereafter be for all purposes the certificate provided for by this act.

Sec. 26.   (Parties to Actions.)   A contributor, unless he is a general partner, is not a proper party to proceedings by or against a partnership, except where the object is to enforce a limited partner's right against or liability to the partnership.

Sec. 27.   (Name of Act.)   This act may be cited as The Uniform Limited Partnership Act.

Sec. 28.   (Rules of Construction.)   (1) The rule that statutes in derogation of the common law are to be strictly construed shall have no application to this act.

(2) This act shall be so interpreted and construed as to effect its general purpose to make uniform the law of those states which enact it.

(3) This act shall not be so construed as to impair the obligations of any contract existing when the act goes into effect, nor to affect any action on proceedings begun or right accrued before this act takes effect.

Sec. 29.   (Rules for Cases Not Provided for in this Act.)   In any case not provided for in this act the rules of law and equity, including the law merchant, shall govern.

Sec. 30.[1]   (Provisions for Existing Limited Partnerships.)   (1) A limited partnership formed under any statute of this state prior to the adoption of this act, may become a limited partnership under this act by complying with the provisions of Section 2; provided the certificate sets forth

(a) The amount of the original contribution of each limited partner, and the time when the contribution was made, and

(b) That the property of the partnership exceeds the amount sufficient to discharge its liabilities to persons not claiming as general or limited partners by an amount greater than the sum of the contributions of its limited partners.

(2) A limited partnership formed under any statute of this state prior to the adoption of this act, until or unless it becomes a limited partnership under this act, shall continue to be governed by the provisions of [here insert proper reference to the existing limited partnership act or acts], except that such partnership shall not be renewed unless so provided in the original agreement.

Sec. 31.[1]   (Act [Acts] Repealed.)   Except as affecting existing limited partnerships to the extent set forth in Section 30, the act (acts) of [here designate the existing limited partnership act or acts] is (are) hereby repealed.

[1] Sections 30, 31, will be omitted in any state which has not a limited partnership act.

Index

Index

OPEC, 178
Operating cost analysis, 25, 117
Orange grove partnerships, 206
Organization expenses, 25, 121,
    147, 186, 196, 209
Overriding roylaties, 181

P

Participating loans, 140
Passive loss provision, 16-17
Pay-in (limited partners), 124, 148,
    187, 197, 209
Percent in ground, 183
Phantom income, 157
Points, 143
Preferential returns, 94
Present value analysis, 56
Principal repayment, 144
Private placements, 85
Product life cycle theory, 193
  pioneering stage, 193
  expansion stage, 193
  stabilization stage, 193
  decline stage, 193
Pro forma analysis, 71, 96
Program sales, 202
Property appraisals, 111-116
  market comparison approach,
    111
  income approach, 111
  cost approach, 114
Prospectus (also see private
    placement memorandum), 85
  estimated use of proceeds, 91
  investment objectives and
    policies, 91
  project description, 92
  sources of invested capital, 92
  partnership allocations, 94

  compensation to general
    partners, 95
  management history and prior
    records, 95
  pro forma estimates, 96
  project risks, 97
  tax aspects, 98
  limited partnership agreement,
    99
  suitability standards, 99
  subscription documents, 100
Proven reserves, 175
Public offerings, 176
Purchasing power risk, 144

R

Real estate limited partnerships,
    105-106, 110, 160
Recourse debt, 32, 93
Real estate syndications, 127
Rehabilitation tax credits, 120
Regulation A, 87
Regulation D, 87-88
Required rate of return, 64
Research and development
    partnerships, 191
Residuals, 155, 164, 167-168
Revenues, 23
Revenue analysis, 115, 178
Return on equity analysis, 29
  Reversion, 123
Roll-in, 7
Roll-out, 7
Roll-up, 7
Royalties, 176, 181

S

Screening Characteristics, 4, 5
Securities and Exchange
    Commission, 86

Index